D1473965

A. B. Marx was one of the most important German music theorists of his time. Drawing on idealist aesthetics and the ideology of *Bildung*, he developed a holistic pedagogical method as well as a theory of musical form that gives pride of place to Beethoven. This volume offers a generous selection of the most salient of his writings, the majority presented here in English for the first time. It features Marx's oft-cited but little understood material on sonata form, his progressive program for compositional pedagogy, and his detailed critical analysis of Beethoven's "Eroica" Symphony. These writings thus deal with issues that fall directly among the concerns of mainstream theory and analysis in the last two centuries: the relation of form and content, the analysis of instrumental music, the role of pedagogy in music theory, and the nature of musical understanding.

CAMBRIDGE STUDIES IN MUSIC THEORY AND ANALYSIS

GENERAL EDITOR: IAN BENT

MUSICAL FORM IN THE
AGE OF BEETHOVEN

CAMBRIDGE STUDIES IN MUSIC THEORY AND ANALYSIS

TITLES IN THIS SERIES

MUSICAL FORM IN THE AGE OF BEETHOVEN

SELECTED WRITINGS ON THEORY AND METHOD

A. B. MARX

Edited and translated by
SCOTT BURNHAM
Princeton University

CAMBRIDGE
UNIVERSITY PRESS

PUBLISHED BY THE PRESS SYNDICATE OF THE UNIVERSITY OF CAMBRIDGE
The Pitt Building, Trumpington Street, Cambridge CB2 1RP

CAMBRIDGE UNIVERSITY PRESS
The Edinburgh Building, Cambridge CB2 2RU, United Kingdom
40 West 20th Street, New York, NY 10011-4211, USA
10 Stamford Road, Oakleigh, Melbourne 3166, Australia

First published 1997

Printed in the United Kingdom at the University Press, Cambridge

Typeset in Bembo

A catalogue record for this book is available from the British Library

Library of Congress cataloguing in publication data

Marx, Adolf Bernhard, 1795–1866
[Selections. English]
Musical form in the age of Beethoven: selected writings on theory
and method / A. B. Marx; edited and translated by Scott Burnham.
p.   cm. – (Cambridge Studies in Music Theory and Analysis; 12)
Includes bibliographical references and index
ISBN 0 521 45274 0 (hardback)
1. Music–Theory–19th Century.   2. Music analysis.
I. Burnham, Scott G.   II. Title.   III. Series.
MT6.M313   1997
781'.09'034–dc20   96–49875   CIP MN

ISBN 0 521 45274 0 hardback

AH

For Allan Keiler

CONTENTS

x   Contents

FOREWORD BY IAN BENT

Theory and analysis are in one sense reciprocals: if analysis opens up a musical structure or style to inspection, inventorying its components, identifying its connective forces, providing a description adequate to some live experience, then theory generalizes from such data, predicting what the analyst will find in other cases within a given structural or stylistic orbit, devising systems by which other works – as yet unwritten – might be generated. Conversely, if theory intuits how musical systems operate, then analysis furnishes feedback to such imaginative intuitions, rendering them more insightful. In this sense, they are like two hemispheres that fit together to form a globe (or cerebrum!), functioning deductively as investigation and abstraction, inductively as hypothesis and verification, and in practice forming a chain of alternating activities.

Professionally, on the other hand, "theory" now denotes a whole sub-discipline of the general field of musicology. Analysis often appears to be a subordinate category within the larger activity of theory. After all, there is theory that does not require analysis. Theorists may engage in building systems or formulating strategies for use by composers; and these almost by definition have no use for analysis. Others may conduct experimental research into the sound-materials of music or the cognitive processes of the human mind, to which analysis may be wholly inappropriate. And on the other hand, historians habitually use analysis as a tool for understanding the classes of compositions – repertories, "outputs," "periods," works, versions, sketches, and so forth – that they study. Professionally, then, our ideal image of twin hemispheres is replaced by an intersection: an area that exists in common between two subdisciplines. Seen from this viewpoint, analysis reciprocates in two directions: with certain kinds of theoretical inquiry, and with certain kinds of historical inquiry. In the former case, analysis has tended to be used in rather orthodox modes, in the latter in a more eclectic fashion; but that does not mean that analysis in the service of theory is necessarily more exact, more "scientific," than analysis in the service of history.

The above epistemological excursion is by no means irrelevant to the present series. Cambridge Studies in Music Theory and Analysis is intended to present the work of theorists and of analysts. It has been designed to include "pure" theory – that is, theoretical formulation with a minimum of analytical exemplification; "pure" analysis – that is, practical analysis with a minimum of theoretical underpinning; and writings that fall at points along the spectrum between the two extremes. In these capacities, it aims to illuminate music, as work and as process.

However, theory and analysis are not the exclusive preserves of the present day. As subjects in their own right, they are diachronic. The former is coeval with the very study of music itself, and extends far beyond the confines of Western culture; the latter, defined broadly, has several centuries of past practice. Moreover, they have been dynamic, not static, fields throughout their histories. Consequently, studying earlier music through the eyes of its own contemporary theory helps us to escape (when we need to, not that we should make a dogma out of it) from the preconceptions of our own age. Studying earlier analyses does this too, and in a particularly sharply focused way; at the same time it gives us the opportunity to re-evaluate past analytical methods for present purposes, such as is happening currently, for example, with the long-despised methods of hermeneutic analysis of the late nineteenth century. The series thus includes editions and translations of major works of past theory, and also studies in the history of theory.

The very look of A. B. Marx's writings conveys the man himself. Just open his manual of composition: the bubbling energy, the drive, the vitality radiates off the page at you! For a start, there is no Gothic script in sight; it is all in a simple, modern-looking, purposeful Roman typeface. And there is the prose: robust, direct, forceful, with short, incisive paragraphs, bursting with emphases. Then there is the layout: sentences frequently broken by dashes to interject asides, the most important words and phrases set out at the center of the line, usually without punctuation, and tabulations summing up each stage of argument. Here he is, for example, at work on rondo forms:

This realization takes us on to the *fifth* rondo form.

Its *first characteristic* is that it strengthens the union of main and subsidiary sub-ject, such that that union stands

as one distinct part

of the the total composition. This part closes with, or after, the subsidiary subject: how - we shall see that later on. Then comes the second subsidiary subject

as second part,

and the last repetition of the main and first subsidiary subject

as third part,

the whole having consequently the following form:

I	II	III
MS SS1	SS2	MS SS1

In addition, text flows into and out of music examples as if music itself had become an integral part of verbal syntax and notation a constituent of the alphabet. Scott Burnham, in his translation, has quite rightly toned down passages like the above by stripping away the rhetorical typography, but I wanted momentarily to reveal to the reader the origi-nal effect (of a passage, incidentally, that does not appear in his selection), while conceding, alas, that to our modern eyes these devices produce only a manic effect.

Marx is perhaps the most maligned – the most *unjustly* maligned – of all nineteenth-century writers on music. Far from being a dry theorist, he is a writer of burgeoning enthusiasm. Far from being a pedant, he floods his writings with a sense of the music that he describes. By no means the mechanical formalist he is made out to be, he in fact portrays a musical world of infinite variety governed by endlessly fluid organic processes. Far from being merely a pedagogue, he is a man of broad-ranging intellect, a thinker who seeks to penetrate to underlying causes. He is a man of many parts: not only a theorist, but also a critic, editor, composer, analyst, biographer, writer on diverse topics, innovative educationalist, polemicist, and progressive thinker, not to mention pro-fessor at one of the greater universities, and co-founder of a musical conservatory.

His role in the nineteenth century's understanding of Beethoven can-

not be overestimated. Marx was a lifelong advocate of that composer's
music. A reviewer of early performances, he went on to treat Beethoven's music as a "universe" for his teaching, drawing constantly on the
works to illustrate matters of harmony, construction, form, and expression. At the end of his life, he produced his two-volume musical biography of the composer, which sought to discover not technicalities but the
spirit that infused Beethoven's music. In short, he did much to shape an
image of Beethoven that has prevailed not only for the second half of
the nineteenth, but also for much of the twentieth century.

His manual of composition, in four volumes, was probably the most
influential work of its kind in the last century. It was a pioneering work,
the father of all music textbooks, the first designed for classroom use as
well as for private study – a new kind of teaching tool. It went through
more editions than any comparable work, spanning 1837 to 1910, and
its first volume was translated into English *twice*. Marx's analyses of the
Beethoven sonatas (1863) were widely distributed not only in Germany
but also on the English and American markets. But on the whole, he was
not served well with translations. The later volumes of his composition
manual have remained untranslated, as have many music criticisms, and
his Beethoven study, to this day. The reader of the present book, beautifully translated and skilfully introduced by Scott Burnham, is in for
many delights and pleasures as he or she explores the capacious and
resourceful mind of this fascinating and quintessentially nineteenth-
century writer.

PREFACE

The musical thought of Adolph Bernhard Marx has long been one of the familiar themes of German musical scholarship, from Eduard Krüger's perennially shared view of Marx's work as Hegelian, through Hugo Riemann's frequently polemical engagement with Marx's method, to Carl Dahlhaus' ever renewable fascination with Marx and his *Formenlehre*. Until very recently, however, there has been precious little in English on Marx, and until this very volume, precious little Marx in English. In the nineteenth century, four of his works received English translations relatively quickly after their initial publication: *General Music Instruction, The Music of the Nineteenth Century, Introduction to the Interpretation of the Beethoven Piano Sonatas*, and the first volume of his composition treatise. Since then, there have been no further translations, despite a burgeoning interest on the part of Anglo-American musicologists in Marx's theory of form, and particularly his view of sonata form.

Thus when Ian Bent invited me to contribute a volume on A. B. Marx to his Cambridge Studies in Music Theory and Analysis, my first thought was to do a translation. But which work of Marx's would be most useful to English-speaking historians of theory? At four volumes, his treatise on composition is impracticably long, whereas his *General Music Instruction*, although compact, does not present his thought at its most developed. And the polemical monograph, *The Old School of Music in Conflict with our Times*, while presenting a fascinating view of nineteenth-century music theory and pedagogy, does not touch on Marx's theory of musical form. My solution has been to translate broad excerpts from several of these works and others, in order to present aspects of Marx's theoretical thought that are of continuing interest today: his progressively designed pedagogical method, his theory of musical form (and particularly sonata form), and his analytical work on the music of Beethoven.

My work on this volume was enhanced by several very special people. First among these is Ian Bent, who, in his wisdom, patience, and generosity, both fostered this project and helped ensure the ideal conditions for its completion. He will always serve as a model to me for how one may best counsel and encourage the work of younger colleagues. Brian Mohr was a great help in the early stages of this project, collating and comparing various editions of Marx's works. Juliet Palmer did a wonderful job copying the music examples. And many thanks to Irene McElroy for her eleventh-hour heroics in helping me produce the manuscript. It was a great pleasure to experience and benefit from the resourceful energy of Penny Souster and the genial professionality of Kathryn Puffett at Cambridge University Press. As always, the indulgence and support of my wife Dawna Lemaire has never flagged, despite its all too infrequent acknowledgement.

Finally, I will always associate A. B. Marx with the atmosphere and circumstances of a graduate seminar on the history of nineteenth-century theory which took place in the spring of 1983 at Brandeis University. There, in the expansive company of fellow graduate students David Cohen and Michael Schiano, I first met Marx, his *Idee*, and his theory of forms. It is in mind of that happy season of friendship and intellectual stimulation that I dedicate this volume to the person who directed that seminar and without whom I never would have been introduced to the headier challenges of the history of music theory, much less to A. B. Marx.

INTRODUCTION: MUSIC AND SPIRIT

We are only now beginning to perceive the full extent of Adolph Bern-hard Marx's presence in nineteenth-century musical thought. A novelist seeking to bring that age and its thought to life would be hard pressed to invent a more appropriately fascinating figure. Although not destined to realize his early dreams of becoming a great composer, Marx was all things else: brilliant conversationalist, fierce polemicist, provocative critic and editor, active participant in a newly galvanized intellectual and cultural milieu (Berlin, shortly after the founding of the University of Berlin), advocate of Beethoven and the first theorist to address the chal-lenge of that composer's music in a comprehensive fashion, systematic yet poetic thinker and writer, progressive pedagogue involved in Prus-sian educational reform, and the author of books on Gluck, Beethoven, composition, pedagogy, cultural criticism, music history, tone painting, and even vocal technique. What made this range of enterprises possible was a world view that entailed, above all, a single-minded sense of mis-sion. For Marx drew energy and focus from his self-imposed calling, which was nothing less than helping to usher in a new age of music and musical understanding, and then working to preserve its glory. His writ-ing is replete with the heady bombast and brimming high-mindedness that such a task so often invites and perhaps even requires.

Any calculated selection of writings from an author as prolific and many faceted as Marx is bound to represent a degree of tendentiousness. The present volume will necessarily neglect several greatly important strands of Marx's enterprise as a musical thinker in the nineteenth cen-tury. These include many of his views on opera, music criticism, and music history. The broader strokes of some of these views will of course be inferable from the material selected for this volume, for Marx's sys-tem of thought is such that any one facet implies and reflects all the others.

1

Marx is certainly best known – and has been since the mid-nineteenth century – as the theorist who named and codified sonata form. This reputation alone might justify the extent to which this volume devotes itself to his theory of form, though few would argue for this particular claim to our attention today without immediate qualification, now that the contributions to formal theory of Koch, Czerny, Reicha, Birnbach, and others have been well charted. More important are the broader issues that the writings in this volume confront, issues that have haunted mainstream theory and analysis for the last two centuries: the relation of form and content, the analysis of instrumental music, the role of pedagogy in music theory, the nature of musical understanding, and, not least, the attempt to understand the music of Beethoven. This last aspect of Marx's agenda surely touches at the root of our own theoretical concerns. For in choosing to base the most important elements of his conception of music on a composer whose works are still regarded as models of organic coherence, Marx defined the nature of musical unity and continuity in terms that remain influential today. But there exists an interpretative motivation for concentrating on Marx's theory of form and compositional method as well, for it is here that he fulfills most explicitly the aesthetic and moral compact that marks him as a member of the Idealist generation; it is here that he sees himself engaged in the great project of elucidating and promoting the union of music and spirit.

The writings in this volume present Marx as a music theorist who deals unflinchingly with two imposing features of the early nineteenth-century cultural landscape in Germany: the metaphysical attitude toward art of the post-Kantian generation of philosophers and literary artists, and the music of Beethoven. Marx's belief in the inwardly spiritual nature of artistic education and expression informs the entire range of his work, from his early essays and reviews in the *Berliner allgemeine musikalische Zeitung*, undertaken in the first fine blaze of Idealism's star, to the bitter ruminations in his last work, *Das Ideal und die Gegenwart* (1867), when that star was no longer the only fire in the sky.[1] And the music of Beethoven is never far away from this central preoccupation; indeed, this music served Marx throughout his career as the first best demonstration of his aesthetic idealism.

For Marx, the ascendancy of art into the realm of the spirit carried with it a moral imperative. This found expression in his renewed em-

---

[1] Published posthumously by Marx's wife, Therese.

phasis on *Bildung*, on the value of a sound education for the cultural well-being of the individual and of the German nation. The seat of this particularly Prussian view of art as an agent of the moral force of the state was the city of Berlin.

Home of E. T. A. Hoffmann, Bettina von Arnim, Clemens Brentano, and a newly founded university, Berlin was a city in cultural ferment, flush with the recent triumphs of German culture and full of future. The founding of the University in 1810 symbolized the union between state and culture. This merger of state and cultural mission – of aesthetic theory and politics – forms perhaps the defining chapter in the construction of the German "spiritual nation." And music's privileged role in this vision of national unity cannot be overestimated, particularly the music of Beethoven and his immediate predecessors. The subsequent reception of Beethoven might well have been different had it not been for two influential documents that, interestingly enough, also stem from Berlin in 1810. I refer to E. T. A. Hoffmann's famous review of the Fifth Symphony, and Bettina von Arnim's infamous letter to Goethe about Beethoven (later published in her book *Briefwechsel mit einem Kind*). Both these documents characterize Beethoven as the epitome of Romantic creativity: Hoffmann seeks and finds in the music the same kind of deep continuity and Romantic vision that literary critics were celebrating in the works of Shakespeare and Goethe, and von Arnim factitiously records a conversation with Beethoven in which the composer expresses himself in accordance with her vision of the Romantic artist. These writings represent some of the first, and best known, steps in a process of literary lionization of the composer while he was still alive.[2] Thus the city of Berlin, as one of the last bastions of German Romanticism, and the home of both Hegelian Idealism and Prussian nationalism, was already in the process of transforming the southern currency of the Viennese musical masters into a more fiercely northern intellectual and political capital. A. B. Marx would play a crucial and abiding role in this enterprise.

Marx arrived in Berlin sometime before 1822. He had come to Berlin to further a career in jurisprudence while seeking a base for his ambitions as a composer and musical thinker. Thus it was no surprise that his path soon crossed that of E. T. A. Hoffmann, then a high-ranking coun-

---

[2] For an engaging account of this process see Charles Rosen, *The Frontiers of Meaning: Three Informal Lectures on Music* (New York: Hill and Wang, 1994), chap. 2 ("How to become immortal").

cillor in the Berlin legal establishment, as well as a composer, music critic, conductor, and – last but far from least – writer of popular stories and novels. Sadly enough, they had little personal contact before Hoffmann's death in 1822. Marx's first substantial publication was an appreciation of Hoffmann's role as a composer and musical thinker, an essay which he wrote in 1823 as an appendix to Julius Hitzig's posthumous biography of Hoffmann. Marx's laudatory discussion of Hoffmann establishes some of the most vital themes of his own work, which was soon to get underway.

In the following year, 1824, the Berlin music publisher Adolph Schlesinger appointed the approximately thirty-year-old Marx as head editor of a new music periodical, the *Berliner allgemeine musikalische Zeitung*, a weekly newspaper which Schlesinger hoped would compete with the ever popular *Leipzig allgemeine musikalische Zeitung*. Given Marx's lack of journalistic experience, Schlesinger's choice was something of a gamble, and the young man's inexperience did in fact manifest itself in an ongoing inflexibility concerning just who was entitled to practice criticism. Marx thought that only composers were fit to pronounce upon music; his stubbornness on this account dried up some of the usual sources of information vital to a periodical of this sort, a situation which gradually worsened and eventually helped bring about the demise of the paper after a seven-year run.

And yet Marx's inexperience held a signal advantage that far outweighed any drawbacks: by not coming from an established journalistic tradition, Marx could more easily create a new ideal for the musical journal. Rather than concentrating on the detailed reporting of musical events, Marx's paper would provide a forum for higher-minded issues – it would treat music as a vital part of cultural and intellectual *Bildung*. Most importantly, the *Berliner allgemeine musikalische Zeitung* would prepare the public for a new age in musical art. According to Marx's inaugural editorial, while the Leipzig paper simply confirms existing public attitudes, the Berlin paper must first awaken and then strengthen the insights necessary for understanding the new age and anticipating the future. It is no coincidence that such a note should be sounded in Berlin at this time.

Marx's writings and ideas found ample resonance in Berlin's intellectual community. During his years as editor of the music journal Marx became an habitué of the Haus Mendelssohn, through which he cultivated the acquaintance of many of the city's most distinguished intellectuals and artists. His skill as a conversationalist kept the teenaged Felix entranced, and the two were great friends for a number of years – until they shared critiques of each other's oratorios, at which point the younger composer could no longer disguise his opinion of Marx's compositional mediocrity.[3] Perhaps the greatest monument of their short-lived but intense friendship was the famous rediscovery and performance of the Bach St. Matthew Passion in 1829. Mendelssohn resurrected the work and conducted the performance, while Marx's professional enthusiasm for the work was instrumental in convincing Adolph Schlesinger to publish it.

By 1830 Marx was enough a part of the cultural mission of the city that he was offered a chair in music at the recently founded University of Berlin (he had also just received a doctorate from the University of Marburg). True, the post had been offered initially to the twenty-one-year-old Mendelssohn, who turned it down and recommended Marx;[4] even so, the offer stands as powerful testimony to the level of esteem Marx had managed to engender in such a short time. For Berlin took its university very seriously indeed. The university came to represent nothing less than the Prussian institutionalization of German Romanticism and Idealism. If the original charter of the university was drawn up by Wilhelm von Humboldt in accordance with the Romantic spirit of Jena (the Jena of Tieck, Novalis, and the Schlegel brothers), others soon envisioned the school as "an institution by, of, and for the state."[5] In its inaugural year, the university boasted a spectacular faculty, including the philosopher Fichte, the theologian Schleiermacher, and the philologist F. A. Wolf. G. W. F. Hegel began teaching there in 1818.

Hegel's lectures were very well attended, and his influence soon became enormously pervasive. Michael Ermarth, in his book on Wilhelm Dilthey, quotes a witness of the period:

For many of us today, the memory is still fresh of a time when all learning lived off the rich table of Hegelian wisdom, when all the other academic faculties waited in the antechamber of the philosophical faculty in hopes of appropriat-

[3] The resultant falling out included the melodramatic scene of Marx's tossing the fragments of Mendelssohn's letters into the lake in the Tiergarten. See George R. Marek, *Gentle Genius: The Story of Felix Mendelssohn* (New York: Funk and Wagnalls, 1972), 109. Marek also documents Zelter's jealousy of Marx's friendship with Mendelssohn (see 112–13).
[4] Ibid., 171.
[5] Theodore Ziolkowski, *German Romanticism and Its Institutions* (Princeton: Princeton University Press, 1990), 299.

ing something from the inspection of the Absolute and from the infinitely
supple Dialectic – a time when one was either a Hegelian or a barbarian and an
idiot . . . when, in the eyes of the Prussian educational and cultural ministry, it
was almost a crime not to be a Hegelian.[6]

The much-noted Hegelian cast of Marx's musical thought is thus hardly
a surprise.

Marx flourished at the University, lecturing on various topics in music history and repertoire and teaching composition privately. In 1833
he was named to the post of university Music Director (which had been
held most recently by Zelter).[7] Marx's successful experiences as a teacher of composition encouraged him to publish what would become his
best-known work, *Die Lehre von der musikalischen Komposition, praktisch-
theoretisch* [*A Practical and Theoretical Guide to Music Composition*]. This
four-volume compositional method went into many editions; an English translation of the first volume appeared in 1852.

Marx's method is very much in line with the pedagogical mandate of
the University of Berlin, as expressed in writings by Fichte, Schleiermacher, and others. This mandate and its application are made clear in
the excerpts comprising Part I of the present volume, entitled "Music
Theory as Education of the Spirit." In the excerpts from his 1841 polemical tract *Die alte Musiklehre im Streit mit unserer Zeit* [*The Old School
of Music in Conflict with our Times*], Marx portentously defines his age in
terms of an apocalyptic struggle between spirituality and materiality.
And by means of his compositional method, he proposes to show how
music can project spirit through its very materiality. His project is thus a
kind of empirical idealism: through experience to spirit. By dint of this
emphasis, especially in light of its Prussian context, Marx's
compositional method becomes a culturalizing and moralizing force. As
the excerpted passages will show, Marx himself unabashedly associates
his work as a music pedagogue with the highest moral aims of the age,
proclaiming the ascension of music instruction from the realm of training to that of cultural education, of *Bildung* in its most exalted sense.

At the heart of Marx's pedagogical method is a respect for the integrity of the student and the integrity of the artwork. He thus refrains
from the artificial separation of musical elements in his treatise, since
such separation is not a condition of actual artworks. And because the

---

[6] Michael Ermarth, *Wilhelm Dilthey: The Critique of Historical Reason* (Chicago: University of
Chicago Press, 1978), 51.
[7] Marx, *Erinnerungen: Aus meinem Leben*, 2 vols. (Berlin: Otto Janke, 1865), vol. 2, 187.

successful creative artist engages his entire being, Marx associates the study of composition with the *Erziehung*, or total upbringing, of the student. Like the programmatic goal of the ideal German romantic university, Marx's approach to the teaching of music stresses *Erkennen* over *Lernen*, active cognition over reactive learning.[8] Education was less a matter of giving information to a student and more a matter of drawing something out of a student's own spiritual capabilities. Self-motivated education was the watchword; of this no student was considered incapable.[9]

Drawing perhaps on the work of the progressive Swiss pedagogue Johann Heinrich Pestalozzi, Marx instituted a method which starts from the contemplation of concrete examples and proceeds to the recognition and understanding of inner laws. Marx's method progresses organically, from simple forms to more complex ones. At every stage the student is alternately encouraged to examine a new formal possibility and then to emulate it (a process that relates to the Goethean polarity of *Anschauung und Tat*[10]). There is no introduction of new material (harmony, etc.) without the immediate application of that material within an actual musical structure, no matter how simple. For example, instead of introducing all the possible triadic resources of a key center and then encouraging the student to use these sounds, Marx shows the student only the most necessary harmonies first (tonic and dominant). Only after the student masters simple two-voice periodic constructions with these two harmonies are the other chords of a key introduced. There is no compositional exercise that does not involve the composition of a total form, however small. This invites an analogy with language acquisition: a developing composer, like a child acquiring language, starts with simple utterances instead of tables of musical and/or grammatical elements.

More important is the overriding concept of totality in Marx's understanding of music and its pedagogy: the student is to be ministered to as a whole person; pedagogical exercises deal with whole utterances rather than the memorization of context-free morphology (chord

---

[8] An emphasis on *Erkennen* rather than *Lernen* was part of the charter for the German university described by Friedrich Schleiermacher in his influential monograph *Gedanken über Universitäten im deutschen Sinn* (1808). See Ziolkowski, *German Romanticism*, 290.

[9] Georg Sowa, *Anfänge institutioneller Musikerziehung in Deutschland (1800–1843)*, Studien zur Musikgeschichte des 19. Jahrhunderts, vol. 33 (Regensburg: Gustav Bosse Verlag, 1973), 33.

[10] See Lotte Thaler, *Organische Form in der Musiktheorie des 19. und beginnenden 20. Jahrhunderts* (Munich: Musikverlag E. Katzbichler, 1984), 67.

charts, etc.); musical works are to be understood as totalities informed
by the composer's entire being; and – finally – critics must exercise their
whole beings in attempting to understand musical works. The ramifica-
tions of this attitude are striking in the context of Marx's treatise on
composition, where it finds expression in the very design of his compositional method. As will be seen in the excerpts drawn from the opening volume of his compositional method, students are enjoined to inter-
nalize the syntax of whole musical forms – however simple – right at
the outset of their instruction, rather than only after a long familiariza-
tion with the nature of harmony and counterpoint. Marx's method proceeds on a spiral path where each stage adds more material to already
established underlying formal procedures.

Marx was not without predecessors in the application of some of
these procedures to compositional method. His empiricism was encouraged to some degree by Gottfried Weber's *Versuch einer geordneten Theorie
der Tonsetzkunst* (1817–21), a work which successfully proposed to jetti-
son the more abstract trappings of eighteenth-century *Satzlehre*, in favor
of a distinctly hands-on approach. And Marx's spiral method was clearly
forecast in J. B. Logier's *System der Musik-Wissenschaft und der praktischen
Composition* (1827), a work which Marx claims to have translated from
the English.[11] But despite the novelty of its method, Logier's treatise
boasts nothing like the range of Marx's own work; the musical contexts
presented therein are quite limited and rather mechanically worked out.

The success of Marx's music pedagogical program earned him an
audience with Friedrich Wilhelm IV sometime in the 1840s. The mon-
arch was very interested in Marx's plans for the betterment of Prussia's
musical life, plans which included promoting the study of authentic
German folk music through the foundation of a Choral School in
which future music teachers and choral directors would be trained. This
institution would be based on the pedagogical principles of Marx's treatise on composition. His audience with the king led to some further
meetings with other important figures, but interest in the initiative
dwindled and then vanished entirely in the explosions of 1848.[12]

Thus Marx's system was never formally institutionalized in Prussia.
Yet that should not obscure the undeniable fact of its influence in the
wider world. Another highly renowned German music theorist, Hugo

---

[11] Marx, *Erinnerungen*, vol. 2, 104–105.
[12] Ibid, 238–47.

Riemann, edited a later edition of Marx's treatise, keeping it alive for German readers. And Marx's reputation as a music educator spread even unto America. Although to my knowledge he was not offered any university positions in this country, he was at one point invited to teach at a prestigious private school in Farmington, Connecticut, known then and now as Miss Porter's School.[13]

Marx's much-discussed *Formenlehre*, his theory of musical form, cannot be separated from his pedagogical method. The basis of Marx's theory of form is a teleological yet ahistorical derivation of musical forms: Marx does not derive later historical forms from earlier forms but rather complex forms from simpler ones. Thus he begins with the four-bar phrase and leads all the way to fully developed sonata form, the form that epitomizes the Viennese classical style. The student of Marx's treatise is enjoined to work through each stage of this derivation, composing ever more complex musical forms, until he or she reaches the culminating sonata form.

Marx characterizes the entire derivation in fine Idealist fashion as the process of artistic reason calling forth its own progressive concretization. And Marx's student relives this process, in the fashion of the student of Hegel's *Phenomenology of the Spirit*.[14]

Underlying the entire series of forms is a disarmingly simple dynamic impulse: Marx expresses it with the formulation rest–motion–rest. At one end of the spectrum, this pattern governs the four-bar phrase in its traversal from opening tonic, through some intervening tones, to a cadential resting point; at the other end, it can be said to inhabit the three large sections of sonata form. In conjunction with this overriding pattern, the concrete musical forms at each stage of Marx's derivation are grounded by a prototypical and highly nuanced dynamic process, subject to innumerable realizations. Marx thus moves away from earlier (and later) notions of musical form as a kind of template, or mold, into which one pours themes, episodes, and the like. His concept of form as a

[13] This fact emerges in an article on Karl Klauser's tenure at Miss Porter's School. Klauser was hired by the school in 1852, after Marx turned down the offer. See *Applause* (Connecticut Public Radio Program Guide) 7/12 (June, 1985), 3. On Marx's influence on a fundamentally important strand of American music criticism, see Ora Frischberg Saloman, *Beethoven's Symphonies and J. S. Dwight: the Birth of American Music Criticism* (Boston: Northeastern University Press, 1995).

[14] See Janet Schmalfeldt, "Form as the process of becoming: the Beethoven–Hegelian tradition and the 'Tempest' Sonata," *Beethoven Forum* 4 (1995), 37–71.

prototypical process is comparable to Goethe's famous work on the
metamorphosis of plants, wherein a similarly conceived dynamic process is subject to infinite realizations, much like the relationship of particular cases to a general law. Ironically enough, one of the most persistent misunderstandings of Marx's theory of form accuses him of being
the fallen angel who first foisted upon us the whole idea of normative
and schematic "textbook" forms.

Part II of this volume, "Marx's *Formenlehre* in Theory and Application," presents the heart of Marx's writing on musical form in general
and sonata form in particular. These writings constitute what is easily
Marx's most broadly known achievement; that they have never been
translated into English is astonishing (and could well be one reason why
Marx's view of sonata form has been so imperfectly understood these
many years). The first selection of Part II is a little-known article dealing
directly with Marx's theory of form. It is revealing that in this exposition
of his theory, written for an interdisciplinary yearbook and thus freed
from the pedagogical demands of his compositional method, Marx per-
sists in presenting musical forms in the same way as in his practical
composition method, i.e. not according to historically-based genre de-
scriptions but in the order of increasing complexity. Thus it might be
argued that such an arrangement not only grants Marx a pedagogical
advantage but must hold some other advantage as well. I have argued
elsewhere that Marx's derivation allows him some striking insights
about the nature of Classical-style formal procedures and their use in
the music of Beethoven.[15] Leading his readers through the rondo forms
to the sonata form, Marx reveals a process of progressive organic integration. Sonata form is thus shown to be the premier form of the age, as
the form which allows the maximal variety within an organically conceived unity. Marx characterizes sonata form as something like an
organism whose subsections function as organs; on the other hand,
"lower" forms (like the Minuet and Trio) have subsections which are
themselves like organisms and thus do not serve a larger totality with the
same degree of integration.

The chapter from Marx's treatise on composition entitled "A closer
discussion of sonata form" presents an extended application of this
theory to musical analysis. In order to demonstrate the dynamic coher-

---

[15] "The role of sonata form in A. B. Marx's theory of form," *Journal of Music Theory* 33/2 (Fall,
    1989), 264–65.

ence of sonata form, Marx discusses each subsection of the form in turn, concentrating particularly on the way each section moves to the next. For this purpose, he uses some twenty sonata-form movements from Beethoven's piano sonatas as models. As Marx takes the reader through different sections of these movements, one often gets the impression of riding along with the composer, stopping at the same forks in the road, and seeing how and why Beethoven steers the course he does. The result is an experience unlike any other in nineteenth-century writing about music.

Marx's treatment of this repertoire demonstrates the analytical efficacy of his fundamental opposition of *Satz* and *Gang*. As prototypical utterances representing closure and open-endedness, respectively, these categories allow Marx to characterize the formal process in Beethoven's music as a kind of energy flow, subject to various checks and enlargements, until it is finally grounded at the end of the movement. Thus Marx's analyses take on a phenomenological immediacy appropriate to that of the music they attempt to elucidate. This is a consequential development, through which Marx becomes the first theorist to trace the processive aspect of Beethoven's music from the perspective of musical form and style. It might even be argued that Beethoven's music made Marx's method and its underlying theory possible. But such things cannot be reduced to a straightforward case of cause and effect. Better simply to observe that Beethoven's music and Marx's theory tend to validate each other. And because Marx's theory of form is intimately connected with his pedagogical method, we can now see a deeper, more implicit role that Beethoven plays in the process of *Bildung* so vital to the Prussian state.

But this does not constitute the full extent of Beethoven's presence in Marx's musical thought: if the Beethovenian sonata form can be said to provide the telos of Marx's *Formenlehre*, then the "Eroica" Symphony surely does the same for his view of music history.

For Marx claims that it was this symphony that brought about the age of ideal music, an epoch that was to become the third and culminating stage in Marx's triadic view of Western music history. Part III of this volume, "Hermeneutic Analysis and the *Idee*," presents both Marx's hermeneutic analysis of the "Eroica" Symphony as well as his view of the historical importance of that symphony. The relevant excerpts are taken from his life-and-works biography of Beethoven, written in the last decade of his life.

Marx's treatment of the "Eroica" Symphony is not without relevance
to his theoretical work. As mentioned above, one of the most characteristic aspects of Marx's musical thought is the interwoven fabric of his
different enterprises, any strand of which (history, theory, criticism, etc.)
implicates and delimits all the others. Thus the entire design of Marx's
theoretical work cannot be apprehended without some exposure to his
interpretative criticism and his view of music history. Moreover, Ian
Bent's recent and already indispensable anthology of nineteenth-
century music analysis has established the central importance of hermeneutic analysis for critics and theorists of that century.[16] We no longer
need to apologize for such analysis, as if it were the poor relation, but
can finally begin to appreciate it for what it was: a synthetic elucidation
less interested in breaking the composition down into its constituent
parts than in seeing the composition steadily and seeing it whole.

In the case of Marx, who never practiced taxonomic analysis, hermeneutic analysis is to be distinguished from the pedagogical analysis he
engages in in his compositional method. Here the goal is not to inter-
nalize a process, as in the pedagogical method, but to interpret a process,
to understand how a piece of music can embody a transcendent Idea.
The concept of the Idea functions for Marx as a token of the presence of
spirit in a piece of music; it provides an index of the marriage of music
and spirit. But the Idea Marx has in mind is not some timeless Platonic
abstraction. In Marx's analysis of the first movement of the "Eroica", the
Idea acts as an emblem of dramatic unity; it is realized by means of a
dramatic narrative. The ability of Beethoven's music to represent such an
Idea is the guarantor both of its own internal coherence and of its culminating position in music history as "ideal music." And *how* it represents this Idea is the subject of Marx's fascinating analysis.

The volume thus concludes by completing the crowning trinity to
which Marx's work tends: Beethoven, ideal music, and sonata form.
Central to the establishment of this trinity is Marx's *Formenlehre*, his
most formidable intellectual achievement and the engine of his teleol-
ogy. The *Formenlehre* may be variously construed: as instruction in composition, as spiritual *Bildung*, as Prussian ideology, and as a validation of
Beethoven's music. The attempt to find a single, dominating motivation
among these choices is difficult and probably wrongheaded. Rather all

[16] Ian Bent, ed., *Music Analysis in the Nineteenth Century*, 2 vols. (Cambridge: Cambridge University Press, 1994).

these motivations mutually and inseparably construct Marx's musical thought.

But we may at least consolidate our view of Marx, for we are now in a position to discern three main streams that come together in his theoretical work: the idealist view of the musical artwork, the pedagogical program of the Prussian state, and an informed brief for the music of Beethoven. This particular confluence was perhaps only possible in Berlin; nowhere else was the urgency to merge the concerns of the state with those of educational philosophy so highly pitched. Add to this the validation and subsequent international glorification of Beethoven,[17] and the result is an inescapably influential paradigm, merging the aesthetic, civic, and moral domains. For without Beethoven, Marx's system of thought would have remained just that: a system. His faith that it was much more than an intellectual contrivance was borne out by his abiding faith in the greatness of Beethoven's music. Beethoven provided Marx with a tangible telos, a point of leverage from which he could construct not only the theory of musical forms but the whole of musical history into a narrative of Hegelian trajectory and sweep.

As the bulwark of a prolifically wide-ranging and fascinatingly situated œuvre, Marx's theoretical writings deserve the additional attention that I hope this volume will inspire. In their marriage of intellectual predisposition, musical praxis, moral orientation, and pedagogical motivation, these writings do justice to the complex grandiosity of their milieu: Europe in the age of Romanticism, the age of music and spirit.

SOME NOTES ON THE EDITING AND THE TRANSLATIONS

I have modernized Marx's often idiosyncratic orthography. He was quite fond of making the typesetting perform something like a rhetorical delivery of his words. This involves indenting rhetorical questions, breaking up sentences so that a single word or formulation could stand

---

[17] The degree of Marx's lionization of Beethoven can never be overstated, and some recent writers – including myself – have claimed that we have indeed underestimated Marx's role in the reception of Beethoven, in the collective construction of the potent mythological figure that has effectively replaced the historical figure. According to one recent study, Marx did more than perhaps any other single person to guarantee the mythologization of Beethoven. See Elisabeth Eleonore Bauer, *Wie Beethoven auf den Sockel kam: Die Entstehung eines musikalischen Mythos* (Stuttgart: J. B. Metzler, 1992).

alone, etc. In addition, he employs both bold face and *Sperrdruck* (spaced type) for emphasis. In the last two cases, I have generally resorted to italics.

My use of different editions for the various excerpts from Marx's treatise on composition merely reflects which editions were available to me at different stages of this project. In any event, the translated excerpts on sonata form from Vol. 3 are nearly identical in the second and fourth editions (the two editions I worked from in Part II); the latter edition restricts its alterations to matters of punctuation and orthography.

I have chosen not to translate the words *Satz* and *Gang*, as well as several of their compounds. Marx uses the word *Satz* to denote a coherent musical utterance at any level of musical form: a phrase, a theme, or an entire movement. I feel it is best to preserve the word in German rather than translate it variously according to its contexts, since the very fact that it can mean a coherent whole at these different levels is crucial to Marx's entire system of thought. For example, throughout much of the section on sonata form in Part II, the word *Hauptsatz* could easily be translated as "main theme" rather than the hybrid "main *Satz*." Yet to do so would lose the inherent connection between phrase, theme, and movement that Marx's use of *Satz* allows. The *Satz* is the vehicle through which his initial formulation of rest-motion-rest is transferred from the most local to the most global musical utterance.

The case for leaving Marx's word *Gang* in German is not as clearly mandated. Yet here I felt that the alternatives were problematic: "run" seems too trivial, and "transition" too specific, too redolent of Anglo-American manuals on form. Moreover, Marx introduces the *Gang* as a complementary opposite to the *Satz*; this opposition provides him with an analytical tool of great flexibility and power, especially suited to the music of Beethoven. It seemed a good idea, therefore, to let both members of this crucial pair of concepts maintain the same profile in the reader's mind.

My decision not to translate *Satz* and *Gang* necessitates the use of the German plurals *Sätze* and *Gänge*, which are undoubtedly off-putting to the reader who has no German. But this is clearly preferable to grafting English plural endings onto these terms and thereby creating awkward sounding words that do not exist in either language.

PART I

MUSIC THEORY AS EDUCATION
OF THE SPIRIT

THE OLD SCHOOL OF MUSIC IN CONFLICT WITH OUR TIMES: SELECTED EXCERPTS

Die alte Musiklehre im Streit mit unserer Zeit
(Leipzig: Breitkopf und Härtel, 1841)

Marx wrote his polemical monograph *The Old School of Music in Conflict with our Times* before all four volumes of his compositional method had yet appeared but after the first two volumes had been successful enough to warrant second editions. The monograph is both a defense of his own compositional method and an attack on the recently published harmony treatise of another Berlin music theorist, Siegfried Wilhelm Dehn.[1] Marx felt he was effecting a revolution in music pedagogy by uniting the traditional divisions of music study, namely melody, rhythm, harmony, and form. He argued that such a union reflects both the unity of the musical artwork and of the unified powers of the student. Dehn, on the other hand, maintained the old divisions and thus drew Marx's fire.

In 1842 Marx's monograph received a spirited response – not from Dehn, but from Gottfried Wilhelm Fink, who lectured on music at the University of Leipzig and was editor-in-chief of the *Leipzig allgemeine musikalische Zeitung* from 1828 to 1841.[2] The debate between Marx and Fink is of great interest and is in fact the subject of an entire monograph by Kurt-Erich Eicke.[3] Much can be learned about the state of instruction in composition and the philosophy of music theory and pedagogy from Marx's critique of Dehn and from Fink's counterattack. Our concern in selecting the following excerpts, however, is with the ambitious programmatic goal Marx sets for the compositional method of the future and how he feels he has met that challenge.

Notable as well in these excerpts is the number of references to contemporary writings (usually German but not exclusively) on psychology

---

[1] S. W. Dehn, *Theoretisch-praktische Harmonielehre* (Berlin, 1840).

[2] G. W. Fink, *Der neumusikalische Lehrjammer oder Beleuchtung der Schrift: Die alte Musiklehre im Streit mit unserer Zeit* (Leipzig, 1842).

[3] Kurt-Erich Eicke, *Der Streit zwischen Adolph Bernhard Marx und Gottfried Wilhelm Fink um die Kompositionslehre* (Regensburg: Gustav Bosse Verlag, 1966).

and pedagogy. These show not only that Marx read widely but that he made a point of keeping abreast of the latest developments in pedagogy.

FOREWORD (DATED BERLIN, 20 MAY 1841)

{vi} With but a single facet of life in our sights, what we are concerned with here is nothing other nor less than the conflict that engages our era and its most noble powers on all sides: it is the struggle of the spiritual against the material, of free understanding against dogma, of irrepressible progress against standstill and stagnation. This conflict is being fought on all sides and in all forms, in politics as in theology, in the sciences and arts as in the foundation of all culture [*Bildung*], the pedagogical and educational system. Everywhere it is a matter of *the spirit becoming free*. But just as the spirit is one and the same in all the manifold variety of its activities, so too its progress toward freedom cannot be one-sided or partial; the true friend of progress and freedom will not underestimate or neglect any direction or enterprise in which this general and urgent struggle is stirring. And herein rests the claim of the musician for a wider audience, one that transcends the inner circle of his art.

The vital question for our art and its influence on the morality and the views of the people is simply this: **whether its spiritual or its sensuous side is to prevail;** whether it is to purify and refresh heart and soul through its inherent spiritual power, enriching the spirit with immortal {vii} treasures, soaring aloft to thoughts and premonitions of all that is highest and eternal – or whether, void of that holy power, it is to weaken and enervate spirit and disposition, burying them in the billows of a narcotic sensuousness and thoughtlessness that dissolves and destroys all that is upright and noble. The art of music is capable of both and has indeed been recognized in both capacities from the earliest ages ...

{viii} The compositional method [*Kunstlehre*] assumes a mediating position between the tone poet and the people, dedicating itself to both and, if art is fully to accomplish its beneficial calling for the people, indispensable to both. Apart from instruction in the technical skills of playing, singing, and so forth, its task is this: to awaken and cultivate a consciousness of musical art and its works. All utterances and activities of the method have only this single purpose, but it is one that conditions and sustains the whole of artistic life. Generally speaking, spiritual cultivation is fundamentally nothing other than a coming to consciousness;

anything that moves us in only dimly perceptible ways subsides with the passing of the moment of excitation and dissolves within the general atmosphere of our existence, unless it is elevated to a conscious {ix} event of the spirit, from which further consequences and effects come forth.

The composer cannot do without this cultivation, this coming to consciousness of his own inner being and artistic experiences, this conscious – and thus beneficial rather than disruptive – assimilation of those things that have already come to pass before him or alongside him in the life of art. It must be emphatically pointed out … that our greatest artists were additionally possessed of educations most propitious for their task, and that, despite the greatest natural aptitude, their works remained defective precisely at those points where some part of the necessary education was lacking. And if anyone still desired to return to that old misunderstanding about the dreamlike unconsciousness of genial creativity, he would find himself corrected not only by the words of a Goethe but by the works and words of the musical masters, namely by Mozart himself – who reveals a remarkably clear consciousness of his intentions and their execution in his letters. But principally speaking, this consciousness can be nothing other than an *artistic* consciousness, one that sets out from *contemplation* [*Anschauung*] and leads to *action* [*Tat*]. In this form it is distinguished from scientific consciousness, which is stamped in a conceptual form; and in both content and form it is an essence completely apart from the abstractions of the reflective intellect, which strove in various ways for validity in the older doctrines of art, and which earned those words of Goethe's, "Calculation is not invention" [Rechnen ist nicht Erfinden] …

{xi} *The compositional method is the first and most important means* … for the sustained triumph of the spiritual … It fulfills this role because it – and when it – comprehends the entire art in all its configurations and relations, because it penetrates and illuminates musical art unto its elements, because it provides instruction and cultivation in artistic form, leads immediately into the life of art and thus founds and maintains the bond between art and knowledge, the amalgamating union of practice and consciousness, and the sympathetic understanding between creators, performers, and receptors. For its lofty task is to bring all this to pass; and truly, it is worthy enough that everyone called to art should stake his complete strength and fidelity to it, and that anyone who has some share in art, progress, and the freeing of the spirit should take a part here as well, with heart and voice – for the time and toil of one man will not suffice to bring it to consummation.

Only after the complete foundation of compositional method {xii} can the history of our art be written: not that ostensible and external history that gives us the empty shells of what has happened in conjunction with chronicles on artists and events, but rather the true history, one that reveals the life and sway of the artistic spirit in artists and their works, and strives to make the divine spirit – eternally one, progressing and prevailing – comprehensible here as well, in this particular series of its revelations.

Only on the basis of a true and complete compositional method is a scientifically exhaustive understanding of art – an aesthetics or philosophy of art – possible. Alternatively, any such treatment that appeared earlier would be obliged to take up the complete practical content of the compositional method.

Only with the assistance of the compositional method can a truly historical or fundamentally scientific treatment of the doctrine of art have any effect; without it such a doctrine would find only listeners and students possessed of an unprepared understanding. It is not the particular fault of our aestheticians and historians if they have not yet been able to complete their task in this sense; to the degree that their work, despite so much worthy strength and dedication, has not been able to reach its end and goal, they bear only the guilt of their age, an age that did not tender them the necessary preparatory and supplementary works. The indispensable middle link between art and science was missing: there was no artistic method.

IMMEDIATE CONSEQUENCES OF THE OLD SCHOOL
(ON THE IMPORTANCE OF TEACHING MELODY)

{29} The lament is old; so too is its answer: melody is a matter of talent; one is born with it; it cannot be taught and exercised.

The answer is old, but it is for that reason not less insipid. It was only devised as a consolation and exoneration by those who have whipped and bestirred themselves and their students down false roads and one-way streets and can no longer conceal the fact that they have led nowhere.

We do not wish to send the old gentlemen forthwith to school with the psychologists, with *Beneke* or *Rosenkranz* or *Michelet*,[4] who would be hard pressed to concede such a thing as an innate melody or a specific spiritual faculty for tone successions and rhythmic motion.[5] We would rather bring them to see boys and girls on the playground, or shepherds in the meadow; or they might listen to one- and two-year-old infants! Anywhere and everywhere they will perceive *song*, pleasure in singing, as the accompaniment of natural well-being; and with small children not yet disturbed by obtrusive foreign influence or a false sense of honor they will even perceive a continuous flow of newly discovered and determined, rhythmicized melodies − that is, *a gift for discovering melody*. Every attentive mother can tell them this, if they will not believe it from me.

With this they may now understand what the psychologist will already presuppose: that the pleasurable gift of one's own song is inbred [*angelegt*] in most people and has already developed to a vigorous bloom in most well-constituted children. And, indeed (as is self-evident), the melodic form is the first of all the musical configurations that man assimilates: only much later does he attain to a comprehension of harmony and even later to his own attempts at harmony. If, nevertheless, most people later show no creative gift for music, no capacity for melodic invention, the reason for this lies in the well-known circumstance that life offers to no single individual time and space enough to develop oneself in all directions; with the seriousness of increasing years, everyone has cause, and feels duty bound, to collect and concentrate themselves for a single purpose, a single direction.

{30} But if *you teachers* deny this primary and lavishly widespread force in your students, wringing your hands instead of helping them along: is it then any surprise that this force in fact fails later on? − And when, instead of cultivating this natural gift, you even steer the tractable spirit of the young apprentice in all directions away from that living path

---

[4] Friedrich Eduard Beneke (1798−1854), who wrote prolifically on psychological and philosophical topics; Karl Rosenkranz (1805−79), who wrote mostly about German philosophy and literature; and Karl Ludwig Michelet (1801−93), a philosopher who wrote about Hegel.

[5] [Marx:] In my *General Music Method* [*Allgemeine Musiklehre*] (2nd edn, pp. 344−49) I have attempted to illuminate, in a popular fashion befitting a book of rudiments, the mostly dark and confused representations of musical aptitude − such as have already brought so many to later grief concerning the care of this aptitude, and have led so many teachers astray, and have served to cloak so much error and neglect on the part of teachers − and then to indicate the natural way to strengthen these aptitudes, to the extent granted to me by reflection and by many years' worth of observations.

unceasingly indicated to every unaffected person by the light finger prods of reason and the presentiment of nature – when you blunt your students with dry rules, render them anxious with eternal prohibitions, feed them with your rows of chords, "that watery gruel of no strength or savor," "let them bite into the sour apple of your misguided counterpoint exercises," and let them "toil themselves to death with the wearying pas de deux of your two-voice fugues, with which you embitter from the outset one of the most profound and most fruitful forms of musical art":[6] then it is obviously no surprise that the majority will have their force broken, and only late or never succeed to that capability and robust facility that was meant for them by nature.

MANDATE AND IMPORTANCE OF THE COMPOSITIONAL METHOD

{8} The art of music lives and works in those regions of life in which the higher activities of the spirit stand in the closest interpenetration with those of the senses. For this reason, no art form works so decisively and so primarily on the sensitive faculty as does music; this is necessarily apparent from one's own experience and that of others. This side of its essence is so predominant, that even great thinkers (Kant, for example) have relegated the entire art to the dim region of the senses, wishing to treat it as a matter of dark and vague taste. In any event, it is undeniable that the majority of people are *primarily or exclusively* capable of gaining from music nothing but *sensuous enjoyment* and that even a large number of musical compositions linger in this region or, after briefly elevating themselves, sink back into it. Only a higher cultivation [*Bildung*] on the part of those receiving and those creating allows them to participate in the higher content that musical art is able to take up and then dispense from within the human spirit. Only this *spiritual content* indisputably elevates music to an art and to a benefactor of mankind. Without this spiritual side, music would be mere sensuous enjoyment, like that afforded by food, odors, the play of colors and lines in a kaleidoscope, etc.; it would be unworthy and incapable of being an object of spiritual cultivation ...

The practice of music demands skills that can be developed to a high degree, indeed to *virtuosity*, and which then presuppose not just certain

---

[6] [Marx:] **Beethoven's** words.

talents but also a high degree of strain and stamina during their acquisition. Thus these skills are *honorable means* toward the ends of art. However, it is only too well known how often they are completely perverted, by virtuosi and dilettantes, so as to become the main affair and thus a vehicle for the mere *vanity of external aptitude.* All too often, as has been experienced in entire schools and periods of art, the true essence of art, its {9} higher spiritual power, is dissipated and killed off by individuals and their vanity. More than once, for ages now, the Catholic Church has fought against this abuse and kindred others; more than once has opera been corrupted by this perversion. So too, for the most part, is the music of the stage and of the home or social circle being corrupted once again.

Thus alongside the *spiritual power* of musical art we see its *sensuous side* and the opportunity it offers even for the promotion of a null and nullifying *vanity.* All this is peculiar to music, and should one wish to ascertain music's influence and worth for the moralization of mankind, it obviously becomes a question of *which of these sides has predominated* or should predominate. If the sensuous and vain side rules, no one will hesitate to deem this degraded art unworthy of such broad and precious participation, or even poisonous and corrupting for the cultivation and strengthening of the people's spirit. Only from its spiritual power may one await a beneficial influence upon individuals as well as upon the life of the people as a whole, may one await a salutary collaboration in church and school, indeed in all the important relations of the inner life.

How and in what sense the compositional method fulfills its task is thus undeniably of general importance – even if we were to grasp it only in terms of its initial vocation, namely as *a liberal school* [*Bildungsschule*] *for creative artists.* How much more important it must appear to us, however, when we convince ourselves

> that it is not just for composers but rather for everyone who wishes to become more deeply educated about music, who wishes to approach music not just sensuously or by some bedimmed groping and guessing but by deeply fathoming its essence – namely that it is the indispensable and irreplaceable means of education for teachers, directors, and other principals of [our] musical institutions.

Perhaps I should have abstained entirely from justifying this declaration. New it is not. Musicians have continually asserted that without such an education [*Bildung*] a fundamental understanding and connoisseurship is not attainable – but when making this assertion they always had before them the prevailing state {10} of theory, the doctrine of harmony or thorough-bass and counterpoint, whose inadequacy we shall consider later.

For now I will simply point out the difference between the circumstances of those who desire cultivation in music and those who desire it in the other arts, in order to illuminate more clearly the necessity of such cultivation.

Literary art speaks to us in words and representations, with which our entire existence from the first awakening of consciousness has made us intimate. The visual arts (leaving architecture – for the most part an external art – to the side) also place figures and appearances before our eyes, of the sort that have long become commonplace through countlessly repeated sightings. One can thus claim that our entire life and the total development of our spirit already act as preparatory instruction for these arts ... Not so our relation to music. Though its initial motions, its elements, coincide with the first impulses of speech and other natural utterances, the connection between these beginnings and the finished art work is so remote and concealed that to comprehend it already presupposes a higher degree of artistic education. And though it goes without saying that we come to hear quite enough music these days, everyone knows how seldom this is connected with a deeper sympathy {11} and, even apart from this, just how little this lump of experience counts in relation to the preparatory instruction that our entire life offers for literature and the plastic arts.

Directly in its external appearance, then, musical art is a much more complex essence than every other art. This is already apparent in that the visual arts are active only in the form of space, and literature only in that of time – the former places its shapes next to each other, the latter lets its representations follow upon one another – while music works in both directions at once, in that it places *next to each other* the tones of a harmony or the voices of a polyphonic piece, and at the same time unfolds one or more series of tones in a *succession* of tones or tunes [*Weisen*]. Moreover, even at first glance one learns what a manifold and complex essence is presented to the eager listener particularly in the case of a larger piece of music, with its great variety of vocal and instrumental forces, with its manifold modulations, harmonies, rhythms, successions of tones, with its voices that now flow alongside each other, now unite, now contend with each other, and yet follow continually their own sense and law.

And to this we may add, finally, *the transitory nature of the musical phe-*

nomenon [*Erscheinung*] – the sorrow of all those friends of art who feel the need to penetrate music more profoundly[7] – through which each of its thousands of moments has already flown away, having hardly struck the listener's senses, while plastic and literary art works stand still for quiet consideration, repeatable at will.

Only compositional method is able satisfactorily to lead one into this world full of figures that are transient, intimate, and yet foreign, and make one feel at home there. This is because it leads the understanding back to the source, to the elements, and from there seemingly recreates the art of music with its unsurveyable army of the most manifold phenomena, allowing it to analyse and explain itself. *No philosophy of art* can {12} enter into such a penetrating discussion,[8] no thinker will find himself equipped for a satisfactory elucidation of art and its works (that is, of its actual life and being) if he himself has not worked through the study of composition in its entirety;[9] even with what seems to me the richest and most rewarding undertaking yet of an aesthetic of musical art,[10] it has necessarily proved to be the case that the execution of an effective aesthetic of music is not at all possible before the production of a complete compositional method.

A more deeply secure comprehension and understanding of musical

---

[7] [Marx:] Hand, for example, in his *Aesthetic of Musical Art* [*Aesthetik der Tonkunst*], Part 1, p. 2, says: "The painting and the statue stand before the eyes and can be considered with a steady fixity of gaze; the work of musical art hovers past, leaving hardly a moment for contemplation." [Ed.:] Ferdinand Hand (1786–1851) taught philosophy at the University of Jena and published the first volume of his *Aesthetik der Tonkunst* in Leipzig in 1837. (The second volume was published in Jena in 1841.)

[8] [Marx:] "Philosophy," says Herbart (*Encyklopädie der Philosophie*, p. 33), while judging its relation to the other disciplines, "may indeed be their servant only insofar as it [prepares] for their principal concepts; *and it will annex itself to them all the better, the more carefully it avoids portraying abstraction as if it were already sufficiently appointed for practical use.*" [Ed.:] Johann Friedrich Herbart (1776–1841) was a professor of philosophy at Königsberg. Marx is probably citing from Herbart's *Kurze Encyklopädie der Philosophie* (Halle: C. A. Schwetschke und Sohn, 1831).

[9] [Marx:] Even Hegel, no matter how broadly he otherwise ranges in his preparatory and supplementary studies, says the following in regard to music (in his *Aesthetic*, Part 3, p. 131): "I am but little traveled in this realm and must for that reason excuse myself in advance if I restrict myself only to more general perspectives and to scattered observations."

[10] [Marx:] The above-mentioned *Aesthetic* of Hand, which shows a diligent and painstaking love of art, may rightly be deemed as such. If I was compelled to raise various objections to its partly inadequate, partly erroneous content in my review of the same (*Hallische Jahrbücher*, 1838, Nos. 281–83), the reason for its defectiveness proved always to be (as I acknowledged repeatedly) only *the impossibility* of attaining a satisfactory understanding without the study of composition, of delivering an aesthetics without the existence of a complete compositional method.

art, a lasting and continually effective acquisition of music's spiritual content – that these things are unattainable without the study of composition we may accordingly assume to be firmly established. For without such preparation one can gain from music sensuous enjoyment, beneficial, indeed even intoxicating and enchanting, sensations, as well as an evanescent train of dreamily aroused feelings and imaginings; but one will never share or be secure in music's highest and most lasting deeds: the gifts that its spirit offers to our own.

{13} Nonetheless, it will ever be possible only for a small minority of music lovers to undertake the study of composition amid their other occupations.

But it is precisely in this connection that one understands the ultimate reason for considering the state of this study and its dissemination as an affair of general importance. If the majority of those of us who love the art can make ourselves familiar with it in no more profound a way than through the practice of singing or playing an instrument, or perhaps only through passive listening and enjoyment, then it must be all the more crucial to us that the teachers to whom we trust our own and our children's cultivation, as well as the officials to whom is entrusted the musical portion of the worship service or the direction of all artistic performances of larger scope, should have acquired the requisite level and breadth of cultivation. Whatever *the individual* expends on music for himself and his circle, whatever *the state* expends on music for its schools, institutions, and churches: as long as the first condition is not fulfilled, namely, *a capable preparation of those who teach and direct*, it is all a risky expenditure that can as easily remain fruitless or even have a damaging effect as be beneficial. When we see music instruction so very often have such little success, when we see it exercise such a diminutive, if not ambivalent, influence on humanity or even on musical cultivation alone, when Rossinian and Bellinian operatic numbers are sung in the Catholic Church at Rome, even for holy occasions, when the Janissary music from Auber's overture to *La muette de Portici* is played in Munich for the procession on Corpus Christi Day, when the Protestant worship service on the one hand rejects any higher role for music[11] (very much against Luther's thinking) and on the other is incapable of comprehending

[11] [Marx:] "In addition to a moral impression, religion makes an aesthetic impression; and this is so essential to it, that *if* it is not to have an aesthetic effect it will have no moral effect at all. For behind the moral concepts, aesthetic concepts are necessarily hidden, as their initial and primary presupposition." Herbart, *Encyklopädie*, p. 85.

higher church music as being an essential part of itself (as was the case in Sebastian Bach's time and later), when (as a complement to the Rossiniades in the Catholic Church) the hunting chorus from *Freischütz* is used to set a text for Advent in a widely distributed collection of songs for schools and other institutions: in all these things we see only individual confirmations of what I have just declared.

COMPOSITIONAL METHOD AND THE COMPOSER

{50} If in the foregoing we have introduced the spiritual content of the art of music, it should not now be difficult to grasp the *task* of the *composer* and the nature of compositional activity.

The composer, who undertakes to conjure up these sensuous and rational figures [*Gestaltungen*] that affect our feelings and our higher faculty of imagination, must naturally possess within himself the same powers with which and on which he wishes to have an effect. Without the activity of the intellect he will not create intelligibly, without feeling he will not be able to divulge and arouse feelings;[12] no one can give that which he himself does not possess.

It is just as self-evident that the different forms in which the spirit is active (sensual perception, intellect [*Verstand*], higher feeling, Idea[13]) merge together as one in the activity of composition − just as their organ, the spirit, is one and the same. They do not become active one after the other, so to speak (now the intellect, now the emotions, etc.). This is in fact what is designated by the word *inspiration* [*Begeisterung*];

---

[12] [Marx:] Goethe told us as much long ago:

> Wenn ihrs nicht fühlt, ihr werdets nicht erjagen,
> Wenn es nicht aus der Seele dringt
> Und mit urkräftigem Behagen
> Die Herzen aller Hörer zwingt.
> Sitzt ihr nur immer! Leimt zusammen,
> Braut ein Ragout von andrer Schmaus,
> Und blast die kümmerlichen Flammen
> Aus eurem Aschenhäufchen 'raus!
> Bewundrung von Kindern und Affen,
> Wenn euch darnach der Gaumen steht;
> Doch werdet ihr nie Herz zu Herzen schaffen,
> Wenn es euch nicht von Herzen geht.

[Ed.:] These lines are from *Faust* I, 534–45. Faust is speaking to Wagner in this passage.

[13] I am adopting Ian Bent's useful convention, in his *Music Analysis in the Nineteenth Century*, of using Idea as a translation of *Idee* and idea as a translation of *Gedanke*.

only a spirit completely filled with and vitalized by its object finds itself in this creative state, the *only* state that can empower the act of creation.[14] {51} And precisely because the *whole spirit is in its highest form of activity* during inspiration, that inspired state is neither unconscious nor dreamy, *nor is it a [condition of] being outside of itself*, but rather is *the deepest inwardness*, the highest *strength of the psychic being*,[15] the highest *consciousness*;[16] that intoxication, that sweet drunkenness of inspiration, betrayed to us by the lips of many a poet, is thus nothing other than the rapture of the soul that feels itself to be *whole and complete* in one Idea or feeling.

Moreover, this state can be aroused from the most various perspectives. At times a thought arriving from elsewhere can stir it; thus, for example, *Beethoven* found his heroic symphony in some enthused thinking[17] about the hero Napoleon (before the latter ascended to the emperor's throne). At other times, a less distinct arousal of one's feelings or even one's senses, indeed a motive encountered by chance, can excite the first spark of a work's life, a work that will come to have infinitely more within it than that first association seemed to promise. It could even be demonstrated, if it were necessary here (every composer who has experienced the power of music in creative hours will testify to this), that even the soberly conceived intention to execute a piece of music in this or that form often ignites, in the process of working on it, a fire of inspiration within the composer's [*Tonsetzer*] spirit, a fire that was not in fact present at the outset, or was only perceived subconsciously, glimmering under the ashes. This process can be seen namely in many works by Sebastian Bach and Joseph Haydn.

{52} This is as much as we will attempt to articulate – only the most

---

[14] [Marx:] Again Goethe: "So fühl' ich denn in dem Augenblick, was den Dichter macht, ein volles, ganz von einer Empfindung volles Herz!" [And thus in the moment that makes the poet I feel my heart is full, completely full with one feeling!"]

[15] [Marx:] Beneke, *Psychologie*, 57. [Ed.:] Marx is probably referring to Friedrich Eduard Beneke, *Lehrbuch der Psychologie* (Berlin: E. S. Mittler, 1833).

[16] [Marx:] Whoever would doubt this could hear confirmation from the mouth of Mozart (in Nissen's biography of him), from Haydn, and from many other artists of the first rank.

[17] [Marx:] But of course if an artwork is to arise, the mere thought, or intention, to portray something will not suffice; rather the artist's previously conceived idea must have become music (and consequently must have been suited to do so). Thus when Herbart (*Encyklopädie*, p. 124) exclaims, "How many artists, even capable ones, are still steered away from the proper path by the prejudgement that their works must mean something or other!" – his words strike only the musician who wants to *express something musically* that is *not musically present within him*.

immediately necessary – about the essential nature of compositional activity. Closer details will of course arise as we proceed.

Only now can we ask:

How must the compositional method fulfill its task?—

And the following is immediately clear:

Just like any method whatsoever, *it must give itself over to [sich dem Wesen zu eigen geben] the essence of that which it would teach.*

Just as philosophy cannot be grasped through memorization, nor chronology through the forms of logic, just as handiwork cannot be learned through purely mental activity, nor a science through physical agility, so musical composition cannot be taught and learned except by means of those mental activities that it brings into application. This is so manifest that I would be loath even to pronounce it, were there not such a long and multifarious history of failure in this regard. Only for this reason is it advisable to investigate this initial precept somewhat more closely.

Let us first keep in mind, as stated above, that composition, the creation of a musical work, is *an integral activity of a spirit completely present to itself [ganz bei sich seiender Geist]*, and that a person's *whole spiritual being*, rather than the merely isolated tendencies of one's spiritual activity (e.g. one's intellect or one's emotion), is what brings forth an artwork. From this I will pronounce the most important fundamental precept for our, or for any, artistic method:

The compositional method must not be content to be a mere system of instruction; it must be an upbringing [Erziehung].

For it does not suffice that the composer possess something, some store of knowledge, or some facility in one or several mental activities: he must possess all those abilities relevant to his task in their highest unity; above all he must be *a complete human being* in his work. A method that {53} does not hold fast to this most important precept, that does not strive with all its powers to turn the spirit of the student toward art as an integral essence by engaging the completely integral activity of that spirit's various faculties; a method that does not, from the beginning, work to awaken and strengthen in the student the consciousness of that inner unity of art and artistic activity, that does not strive, nor is able, to arouse the various active faculties in the spirit of the student to work together, to fuse into one higher collective activity; an artistic method that instead of this preserves and promotes only isolated tendencies of spiritual activity, neglecting or even repressing others: such a method can *perhaps* activate isolated acquirements and abilities, but it will *never* fulfill its actual vocation, never impart or further artistic education. Indeed, it will rather hinder the development of the artist,[18] because it draws its adherents away from the chief condition of artistic creation, the unified oneness of the spirit.

Of course in most cases the business of upbringing cannot be laid completely at the door of the composition teacher, because as a rule it is not given over to him exclusively, that is, from the first youth of the pupil. Yet this is the usual fate of upbringing.[19] Not even the parents, much less those educators and teachers who enter at a later stage, are the exclusive guides for the young pupil – but not one of them will neglect his duty because of this. On the contrary, he will redouble his zeal and his efforts, in order to attain the goal despite foreign influences that now disturb and now lead astray, despite those things that were perhaps neglected or misrepresented earlier on. And how infinitely important, how much more necessary {54} than in most other branches of study this exertion becomes in the study of music; we have already (p. 24) been made to realize how life prepares the way much less for musical training than for training in the other arts and, we may add, for all other spiritual pursuits! How urgently necessary the above demand must overwhelmingly appear to everyone with experience who has also observed how the practical instruction in instrumental playing or singing that initiates our musical training is *chiefly* directed toward introducing external dexterity, in an unbelievable neglect of true training and upbringing – i.e. that which proceeds from inwardness out!—

But how can compositional method achieve this goal?—

Primarily through a vital predominance, *in both method and teacher*, of the *clear consciousness of this unity* – the unity that must be within the composer, just as it is within art generally and in every particular art-

[18] [Marx:] Some words of Tegnér, in a completely different connection (*The Church and School of Sweden*, 1837, p. 138), are also on the mark here: "It is the task of the teacher to ensure that *unity of the spirit* does not get lost in the *manifold variety of knowledge*, that the *human being* does not dissolve and *evaporate in the scholar*." [Ed.:] Marx refers here to the work of Esaias Tegnér (1782–1846), a Swedish writer best known as the author of the *Frithiof Saga*.

[19] [Marx:] Beneke (*Educational Method* [*Erziehungslehre*], Part 1, p. 9): "In addition to the influence of the educator, countless others work together to affect the process of educational upbringing [*Erziehung*]: innate psychical abilities, conditions of the body, environments, and a crowd of chance circumstances." [Ed.:] Marx is citing Beneke's *Erziehungs- und Unterrichtslehre* (Berlin: E. S. Mittler, 1835–36).

work, indeed in every part of an artwork. But this consciousness is not demonstrated and disposed of simply by my maintaining generally that such unity does indeed exist; that would be but an abstract and fruitless assertion, the empty sound of words alone. On the contrary, the consciousness of that unity becomes real and alive when it has penetrated and comprehended all of art, in all its utterances, forms, and works.

Next, in that it challenges the student throughout, as soon and as often as possible, to a completely integral [*einheitsvoll*] process of contemplation and act [*Anschauung und Tat*]. He must create artistically as soon as possible, even if on the smallest scale and with the slightest means. The simplest melody – insofar as it is a true melody – is already an artwork, and it already gives its author a conscious impression of artistic creation and hence arouses or enhances his own artistic capability. Every composition, even the smallest – as long as it originates in this spirit – is a step forward, *not to* the path of the artist but *already on* that path; and it is a new fortification and strengthening of the artistic spirit in the pupil.

Furthermore, in that the student is led to the apprehension of this same spirit in the works of the masters, and that the powerful union of method, great models, and his own {55} impulse and thought elevates the level of his assurance, his mettle, and his powers toward the completion of his life's grand enterprise.

Finally, in that it stimulates and develops not some one or other *but each of the spirit's artistic activities and all of them together,* to the extent granted by motivation and ability.

It may at once be objected that *sensuous perception and feeling* cannot be taught and that the compositional method cannot even hope to arouse them in musical form. Nevertheless, the method can have a significant influence even here, exercising a decisive effect on the entire artistic nature of the pupil through sensuous perception and feeling. It can do this by directing him, through the example of its entire procedure, to act always *with sensuous vitality and a fully engaged soul.* This succeeds when the assignments are of a *thoroughly artistic nature,*[20] when the teacher in-

---

[20] [Marx:] "*Is this possible – and from the very outset?*"— This is what teachers of the old school will ask.— It has been *one of the leading precepts* of my compositional method and (as I permit myself to hope) is worked out even more successfully in the second edition than in the first. Assuming elementary knowledge (systems of pitch, notation, and meter), the method *begins immediately with actual composition,* within *the first hour* of practical instruction with individual students, and

troduces none but artistic configurations, or those that *immediately* become artistic,[21] and when he expresses no doctrine {56} that does not lead *immediately* to artistic application and elaboration.[22]

If a method does not achieve this, it mistakes and neglects, from the beginning and throughout, artistic nature, which itself is not abstracted spirit but living spirit in sensuous appearance. And thus such a method misleads the pupil to the fundamentally pernicious distinction between the sensuous and spiritual existence of the essence of art, from which artistic activity can never proceed and which has occasioned from all sides the most doleful misunderstandings, blunders, and aberrations.[23]

The actual task of the compositional method is of course more comprehensive and materially richer: *to lead to understanding* [*Erkenntnis*]. But *what kind* of understanding is needed by the composer and by anyone at all who would cultivate and instruct himself in the service of an art?—

Only the very smallest part of the knowledge requisite for artistic education is of a merely external sort, in the sense that only intelligence and memory need be present; this includes, apart from the elementary

within the second classroom session in my open courses. It goes without saying that the first assignments are very simple, quite limited in material and extent; but they are of an artistic nature throughout, putting the student *immediately* into artistic activity and into a joyful frame of mind for the matter at hand. I have always perceived the early arousal and steady growth of this state of mind as a heartening requital for my efforts as a teacher.

[21] [Marx:] Diesterweg (*Guide for German Teachers* [*Wegweiser für deutsche Lehrer*], new edition, 1838), p. 133. "*Start from the perceptual* and proceed to the conceptual, from the individual to the general, from the concrete to the abstract, and not the other way round. This axiom is valid for the entire domain of instruction, as it is for general education [*Erziehung*]. *Only through the comprehensive application of this axiom can one succeed in banning all hollow learning, all empty, void, fundamentally harmful, and spiritually weakening play with conceptual forms – play that leads to a blind adherence to misunderstood words, enslaves one spiritually*, and prevents one from coming of age."
[Ed.:] Friedrich Adolph Wilhelm Diesterweg (1790–1866) wrote many books about pedagogy, including works on the theories of Pestalozzi.

[22] [Marx:] If my own work (and my own convictions) were not older than my acquaintance with Diesterweg's excellent *Guide for Teachers*, then I would have taken these his words, from which one of like mind and practice readily perceives a deep vein of experience, and used them as a motto: "**First** [let me say it] **yet again, that I wanted to work against the pale and lifeless tendency of many teachers. Oh, what often cold and soulless pedantic trumpery! What lifeless rule mongering! What propagation of spiritual servitude!**"—

[23] [Marx:] More of this in my *Science of Music*. By the by, it is precisely here that we perceive the origin of those aberrations that we mentioned in note 17, citing Herbart. The *peripheral thinking* about feelings and representations that are not within the music (or perhaps cannot be in music at all) subsides in and of itself *when the whole spirit is within music*. [Ed.:] Marx never completed his *Science of Music*, which he intended as a more strictly theoretical treatment of music. It must have been an ongoing project for many years, since he referred to it in writings dating from the late 1830s to his death.

rudiments,[24] information about the ranges and technical capabilities of instruments and other things of that sort. And even here, such *external knowledge* will remain fruitless and without issue if one does not *enter into the spirit* of the object of knowledge; all the information imaginable concerning the range, handling, difficulties, and simplicities of, {**57**} say, the clarinet will not enable anyone who has not understood the instrument's nature sympathetically, who has not felt and lived along with it, to write suitably for it or even to recognize suitable writing.

In everything else, however, the apprentice of art can benefit only from an understanding [*Erkenntnis*] that rests *on his own* sensuous perceptions and experiences, *on his own* process of examination, one that develops into a conviction. In all other branches of education, this is the method that is truly fruitful and vital. *Art, on the other hand, cannot exist at all without it.* For in the end it is I myself who must hear or see, my own heart that must feel; no one else's eye or ear or soul can replace the relish of my own. So, too, each of us can sing or paint only that which is in one's own soul. It is oh, so sad that one even has to say all this – and to teachers!! — *But with eyes that see they are blind, and with ears that hear they are deaf.* —

Finally, this understanding must not be merely *artistic*, i.e. rooted (as we said above) in the student's own sensuous *perception*, his own inner experience, and his own deepest understanding and conviction, but rather must be *fundamental*.[25] It must connect to the simplest living elements [*Existenzien*], to the *natural material* [*Naturstoff*] of music (sound,

---

[24] [Marx:] As communicated in my *General Music Method* up to p. 126 (2nd edn).

[25] [Marx:] Let us hear still another witness for this truth and for the hundred-year-long aberration of the old method, the insightful H. G. Nägeli in his "Lectures on Music" from the year 1826, thus after the appearance of G. Weber, Logier, and others: "The music-compositional method must give instruction as to how rhythm and melody can be bound together, elementarily and combinatorially, to form an artistic whole. It must achieve this methodically, from the bottom up."
But it has not to this day achieved this, nor has it attempted to achieve this. It has overleapt its simple foundation and contrarily *laid a very compound foundation.* Instead of making the succession of tones its fundamental law, it has done so with their simultaneity, their sounding together. The *doctrine of harmony* was its *foundation,* the *doctrine of chords* its *method.* Melody was *arbitrarily* linked to this and thus made dependent; *rhythm* was treated only *by the by.*— G. Weber, in his new *Theory of Musical Composition,* says quite simply: "Rhythm is not of the essence"!
[Ed.:] The works mentioned in this note include J. B. Logier, *System der Musik-Wissenschaft und der praktischen Composition* (Berlin, 1827), Hans Georg Nägeli, *Vorlesungen über Musik mit Berücksichtigung der Dilettanten* (Stuttgart: Cotta, 1826), and Gottfried Weber, *Versuch einer geordneten Theorie der Tonsetzkunst,* 3 vols. (Mainz: B. Schott's Söhne, 1817–21).

tones, etc.); it must summon up a consciousness of music's chiefly sensuous, but at the same time {58} spiritual, effect; and it must *immediately*
point out and lead to the nearest way in which the spirit makes use of
music for artistic purposes. This first use of music may be as simple as the
linking of three tones or chords in the simplest rhythmic ordering:

Example 1.1

Even so, it is already an artistic usage and as such bears within itself (if
only in the most paltry manner, in seed form) all the relations of the
artistic spirit; here sensuousness, higher feeling, understanding [*Verstand*],
and artistic tendency are already present.

To point this out and then to lead the learner on, through creative
work, to ever deeper insight, ever more comprehensive understanding
and power, and to ever higher, broader, and more characteristic tasks:
this is *the task of the compositional method* and is precisely – I am entitled to
say this, and indeed must say it – *the tendency of my own method.* The
compositional method has fulfilled its task when it has revealed that
spirit which, connecting with nature's given materials and with one's
initial imaginings and formations, progresses *through the whole art [of mu-
sic] in a productive and unified fashion,* right up to its highest tasks – when it
has revealed that spirit and given it the freedom, within the student, to
perform any artistic deed.

2

A PRACTICAL AND THEORETICAL METHOD OF MUSICAL COMPOSITION, VOL. I: SELECTED EXCERPTS

Die Lehre von der musikalischen Komposition,
praktisch-theoretisch, 7th edn, 1868

Marx wrote his famous treatise on composition as a result of his experiences teaching composition at the University of Berlin. The first two volumes were published in 1837 and 1838; they were already in their second editions when he published the next two volumes in 1845 and 1847.

After the foregoing excerpts on the nature and goals of Marx's progressive theory of music pedagogy, the purpose of the following excerpts is to demonstrate its initial application within his compositional method. I have omitted and paraphrased some of the more abstract notions of form that appear in these pages, since Marx handles them explicitly in the essay entitled "Form in music," which can be found in Part II of this volume.

INTRODUCTION

SECTION ONE: CHIEF MANDATE OF THE COMPOSITIONAL METHOD

{1} The compositional method has *first and foremost* the purely practical goal of providing direction for musical composition, of enhancing one's compositional skill – presuming aptitude and practice on the part of the student. It *entirely* fulfills this mandate only when it teaches *everything*, when it enhances *all* the skills that a composer true to the calling is obliged to attain; it comprehends nothing less than the whole of musical art.

To this end it must *first* present an array of *positive information* (e.g. on the technical usefulness of instruments). At the same time, it may presume a certain degree of general education, certain supplemental infor-

mation and skills, and an elementary knowledge of musical rudiments –
or else it may indicate the means to attain such knowledge.

Second, it bears the task of awakening and intensifying the spiritual
capabilities of the student, and *third*, of communicating to the same the
understanding [*Erkenntnis*] and insight necessary for successful musical
composition.

The type of understanding necessary and peculiar to the artist is of a
characteristic nature, as is art itself.

Art is *not* a purely spiritual essence like thought, of which science
must treat, or like faith, which religion preserves in us. *Nor* is it of a
purely corporeal or material constitution. *It is living spirit, revealed in
corporeal/sensuous form* [*Gestalt*]. A method that handed down the abstracted spiritual content of art would no longer be an artistic method
but rather a philosophy of art. A method whose business it was to hand
down the materiality of art apart from its spiritual content would begin
by killing art and would never attain to art's true being and essence. {2}
The task of the rightful artistic method is rather this: to bring this [artis-
tic] essence in all its spiritual/sensuous utterances and relations to the
consciousness of the student and thus to make it his true possession.
Dead material would be an unnecessary burden for him – he would as
little know how to use it as he would the works of a language whose
sense is unknown to him; on the other side, abstracted ideas would
hover past him like gray shadows of a life that has disappeared.[1] It is not
the task of the artist to peer after a now moribund life; his business is
living creation. Not for him, a play with ill understood utterances, de-
void of content; he must rather work with certainty, expressing himself
clearly and distinctly within the world of his art's forms. To this end he
must see into the heart of that world and possess it entirely. No artist has
ever existed, or is even conceivable, without this understanding [*Erkenntnis*] and spiritual assimilation.

SECTION TWO: ITS ARTISTIC TENDENCY

Since the compositional method's chief *aim is purely practical*, that of
enabling one to exercise the art of music, *its form must be thoroughly*

[1] Marx's formulation of the one-sidedness of material vs. the one-sidedness of abstract spirit is
akin to Schiller's dichotomy of the will to form [*Formtrieb*] and the will to material [*Stofftrieb*], as
presented in his famous essay "On the aesthetic education of man." Consequently, the work of
the compositional method, as Marx envisions it, might be something like Schiller's synthesizing
will to play [*Spieltrieb*].

practical and directed toward the essence of art. It may not engage itself in scientific proof (since the activity of the artist is non-scientific), even though it rests on a scientific foundation – just as the artist's work is unconsciously founded on the deepest reaches of scientifically provable reason. The compositional method leaves this final foundation and validation to *musical science.*

Its business is much rather to draw out and illuminate artistic understanding from that most *inward sense and consciousness,* innate to everyone with musical aptitude. It turns first to this immediate sensation and consciousness in the apprentice, which, according to its partly conscious and partly unconscious nature, one may style *the artistic conscience* and which is the first and last guide of the apprentice as well as of the most seasoned artist. Each step of the method, every bit of advice and admonition that it offers can rest only on this understanding [*Erkenntnis*] – for art exists only for itself and is its own law; it can take upon itself only those laws and rules that follow from its own nature.

For this reason, whoever is conscious of a *sympathetic sense for music* can be granted this consoling assurance: *that through this sense he is already capable of comprehending the compositional method in the entirety of its content;* for he already carries in his heart that alone upon which it rests. The method has no other business than to bring this sense to ripe consciousness, by guiding it through the profusion of forms [*Gestalten*] in the world of art, enriching and strengthening it with them all.

ELEMENTARY COMPOSITIONAL METHOD

FIRST DIVISION: ONE-VOICE COMPOSITION

Section One: The first formations [*Bildungen*]

*Tone succession [*Tonfolge*] and its species*

{21} When we consider any piece of music, we notice that it consists of a series of tones or of several such series proceeding together simultaneously; these series are to be performed by one or more voices or one or more instruments.

We begin with the simplest thing, i.e. with a single series of tones; for now, let us call it melody.

But even here we must make at least two distinctions. Every melody contains not only tones that follow each other, but also a specific rhythmic ordering, which dictates *when* one tone is to follow another, *how long* each tone shall last, etc.

Let us again retreat to the first and simplest thing, to the *succession of tones*, leaving its rhythmic ordering to the side for now. We will thus deal chiefly with the content of the tones in the tone succession.

These tones can follow each other in such a way that we can go from lower tones to higher, or from higher to lower, or even back and forth.

Example 2.1

We thus distinguish *ascending* series (a) and *descending* series (b), as well as such series that now ascend and now descend (c), which we call *roving* series. Even the repetition of one and the same tone (d) can be seen figuratively as a species of tone succession. Finally, tones can follow each other *by step*, as in a, b, and c, or *by leap* (e).[2]

{22} One can easily observe that ascending successions awaken the feeling of intensification, elevation, and tension, while falling successions awaken the contrasting feelings of slackening, depression, and the return to rest; roving successions, however, hold fast to neither side of these feelings but partake of both in an undecided fashion, hovering between them. And yet, no matter how their individual tones may roam, they can belong in the main to one of the two primary directions:

Primarily ascending   Primarily descending

Example 2.2

If so, they *primarily* bear one of the respective characters. So much for the direction of motion; on the nature of motion we will observe only that stepwise motion is more restful, more uniform, and more even-tempered, while leaping motion is more fervent, less steady, and less restful. More details will follow.

---

[2] [Marx:] With this we are already made aware of the inexhaustibility of the realm of tones. If we were to restrict ourselves to only eight tones (rejecting all higher and lower octaves, all chromatic alterations, tone repetitions, and series of less than eight notes), it is mathematically demonstrable that we would yet be able to form 40,320 different tone successions. —But it is not for the artist to count and do sums but to be able to invent from a free spirit. It is not mathematics that leads to this end but rather a higher consciousness, or lucid view, of the content of our tone successions.

There follows a section which describes and then analyses the notes of the C-major scale, establishing the "first opposition" in music, that of rest–motion–rest, as expressed in the scale: c (rest)–d e f g a b (motion)–c (rest). Marx claims that this opposition is the fundamental law of all musical formation. (See Part II, p. 97.)

Rhythmicization of the tone succession

{**25**} Up to now we have considered *only the tones* of the tone successions, taking it as granted that they resound for us *one after the other.* This can happen in *equal segments of time* or in *unequal* segments, the latter with great variety. For this reason, let us begin with the first, and simplest, manner, setting the value of each successive tone equally, e.g. giving each tone the length of a quarter note.

Example 2.3

Yet such a temporal ordering of the tones cannot satisfy for long, since each tone comes and goes undistinguished from the others. Were we to let more extensive successions of tones of equal duration pass by without distinctions, the effect would be even less happy; it would be enervating and confusing. Our apprehension hurries to make distinctions, to order things; it leads to a division of the whole series, in order to make it more distinct and comprehensible. The simplest division is by *two*; we begin as follows, thus achieving a metrical division [*Taktordnung*] and, indeed, the simplest such:

Example 2.4

{**26**} Each segment (*measure*) has an equal number of equal tones, and the entire tone succession is contained in four bars – a clear and easily divisible number.

   This metrical division is at first devised only by the intellect, and is visible only on paper. So that it might become noticeable and alive to our sense and perception [*Sinn und Gefühl*], we distinguish the first tone in each division, namely, c, e, g, b, with a stronger address/attack (designated with ^). By means of this stronger accent, the first part, or *main part*,[3] and thus the beginning, of every measure becomes perceptible; at the same time an alternation has appeared in our tone series, introduced by a specific and rational need.

Our tone series now appears completely ordered also in regard to the temporal succession of its tones, and this temporal succession is made palpable and more effective through accent (the alternation of stronger and weaker parts, main and subsidiary parts): the series has thus obtained *rhythm*; it has been rhythmicized.

A tonally [tonisch] and rhythmically ordered series of tones is called melody. Melody is the first real mode of [musical] art; at the same time, it is the simplest. The foundation of tonal ordering will soon be shown more closely.

Already in the case of the tone series that we established as fundamental [Example 2.3], our first concern was that it begin and end with the most important tone, the tonic; its sense of completion and perfection rested chiefly on this. —And now we have also learned to distinguish tones that are rhythmically more, and less, important. If our melodies are to be completely rounded off rhythmically, we must take pains that their initial and final tones, or the latter in any case, be rhythmic main parts and stand out more weightily.

The above melody indeed begins with a main part but does not close with one; the final tone has no accent, and the entire melody seems to die away, since its final tone, as a subsidiary part, carries no weight. Our next task, then, is to provide it with an accent, to transpose it to a main part. We manage this by letting the tone succession appear on the upbeat, as follows:

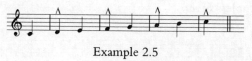

Example 2.5

The initial tone has lost its accent, {27} but the succession of the remaining tones and the satisfying close make sufficient amends.

Yet we cannot remain bound forever to this upbeat model; it must be possible to place *both* initial tone and final tone on main parts.

---

[3] [Marx:] We call the first tone in the bar the *main part* (as my *General Music Method*, p. 107, describes more closely); the rest are called the *subsidiary part*. In compound meters (e.g. 6/8 meter, built from two times three eighth notes), tones that had been the main part in the simple meter, e.g. the fourth eighth note in 6/8 meter, are called the *former main part*.

Here we would like above all to impress upon ourselves *a maxim* that has shown itself to be very helpful in all exertions of the apprentice period and of artistic creation and that is otherwise already applied by everyone involved in spiritual enterprises (even if they are not clearly conscious of it).

When some configuration or other does not appear to us to be completely clear and comprehensible, in all its parts, we want *first* to hold fast to that which seems necessary, or at least, to that which we have recognized to be secure, *whatever it may turn out to be* – and then seek to determine what is lacking.

In the above case the chief task is clear: to place both initial and final tone on main parts. In addition, we have deemed it advisable that the eight tones of our tone succession appear in four bars – indeed we know as yet of no other form. And finally the last tone, if it is to fall on the main part of the last bar, must either be a half note or have a quarter-note rest after it, for without this the last bar would be incomplete. We know all this; on the other hand, we do not yet know how the other tones will be ordered. Let us lay down everything that is known: the division into four bars, the tonic as half note in the last bar, the tonic as main part in the first bar, and at least the outset of the tone succession:

Example 2.6

Now we see clearly what needs to happen: the three missing *tones* must appear in the one still empty space of a bar. The first of these *can* still be a quarter note, while the other two *must*[4] then distribute themselves within the time of the second quarter note; they must become eighth notes.

Example 2.7

---

[4] [Marx:] This is at least the most logical distribution. One could also arrange the third bar with the two eighths first and then the quarter, or with three quarters as a quarter-note triplet, etc.; but [the above version] is more strictly logical and, moreover, does not introduce any essentially new result.

We have thus achieved a tone configuration that corresponds to every demand put forth thus far. It is: {28}

1) satisfying in respect to the succession of tones, in that it begins and ends on the tonic;
2) rhythmically well ordered;
3) unequivocally rounded off, by dint of the accents on the initial and concluding tones, and thus sufficient in this regard.

At the same time, directed only by the needs of the matter at hand, we have attained:

4) *variety* of rhythm, three different durations of the tones: half note, quarter note, and eighth note.

And finally:

5) this variety is demonstrably purposeful. For the final tone, the goal of the whole, has the greatest duration, and the eighth notes immediately preceding it serve to accelerate the motion leading into it and even to make it more characteristically final. Like the tone succession itself, the rhythmic ordering is also one of progressive intensification right up to the conclusion.

We call a melody that is satisfyingly closed off in relation to the content of the tones, as well as to the rhythm, a *Satz*.[5] Examples 2.5 and 2.7 are the first *Sätze* that we have formed.

Up to now we have represented our tone series as always ascending. Why so? — It would have been just as permissible to form descending or roving tone series (see p. 38), but the ascending form lay closest to hand, owing to the usual and natural succession of scale degrees from low to high. Now that we have attained a satisfactory result in that manner, we turn to its opposite, the *descending direction*. And we will indeed execute it in the manner of Example 2.7, thus gaining a *Satz* that is just as consistently and sufficiently formed:

Example 2.8

---

[5] See Introduction, p. 14, for the word *Satz* and the rationale behind the editor's decision to leave the word untranslated. The plural form of *Satz* is *Sätze*.

But only now do we recognize that each of these *Sätze*, Examples 2.7 and 2.8, is one-sided and offers, in this regard, but a one-sided satisfaction. The first merely *rises*; the other merely *sinks*. Only when *joined together* into a greater whole can they offer complete satisfaction in both directions.

Example 2.9

{29} Here we have achieved a formation of tones that undergoes an intensification in tone succession and rhythm from the opening tonic up to a point of satisfaction, the tonic in the higher octave, marks this point with a rhythmic point of repose, and returns from it in just as measured a fashion to the repose of the first tone: *elevation* from repose and intensification in tone succession and rhythm up to a natural *high point*; *return*, likewise with intensified motion (but with a tone succession that now leads to repose), to the true *tone of repose*. We can see that this formation is composed of two halves (a and b), each of which is rounded off and identical to the other in terms of tone content and rhythmic shape. But each half is also clearly distinct from the other in the direction of tone succession; on the other hand, only through this opposition of their directions do they complement each other and belong to each other, as onset and return − a whole, consisting of two subordinate wholes.[6]

We call this sort of musical formation, in which two *Sätze* (*Satz* and opposing *Satz* [*Gegensatz*]) have joined together into a greater whole, a *period*;[7] the first half (a in Example 2.9) is the *antecedent* [*Vordersatz*], the second half (b in Example 2.9) the *consequent* [*Nachsatz*]. Both period

---

[6] This relationship of the complementary combination of two wholes into a greater whole is reduplicated in Marx's famous treatment of first and second themes in sonata form. (See Part II below, pp. 132–34.) For an interpretation of this particular relationship in Marx's work, see my "A. B. Marx and the gendering of sonata form," in *Music Theory in the Age of Romanticism*, ed. Ian Bent (Cambridge: Cambridge University Press, 1996), 163–86.

[7] [Marx:] The question of whether periods can be formed in other ways, with more than two *Sätze*, will be taken up later in the Second Part. For now, only periods with two *Sätze* appear to be conceivable, since we only have two types of satisfying closure so far: the tonic in the higher octave and in the lower octave. [Ed.:] This is a good example of Marx's pedagogical logic: he introduces only one type of period at this point, in accordance with the limited number of cadences he has introduced. But note how he manages to illustrate a fully developed formal type − the period − with a minimum of melodic information.

and *Satz* are distinctly and sufficiently closed off, as self-subsisting wholes; this is their common character. Yet they are different from each other in that the *Satz* has but a one-sided evolution, while the period embraces the other side as well, the opposing side. Up to now, this evolution has been shown only in the direction of the succession of tones: Example 2.7 was a *Satz* that merely ascended one-sidedly; Example 2.8 was a *Satz* that descended just as one-sidedly: the period of Example 2.9 unites both and supplements the one type of one-sidedness with the other.

Could periods also be formed with an opposite shape, with a descending antecedent and ascending consequent? — Certainly; and we will be directed to such things later on. For musical art has so infinitely many moods and representations to express, that it must match these many-sided tasks with equally many-sided means. In general, however – apart from particular and less common tasks – it is natural to begin every communication, musical as well, more restfully and then to elevate oneself out of this restful state to a greater and more incisive zeal, both out of involvement with the matter or feeling at hand and out of a desire to communicate with {30} penetrating effectiveness. Ultimately, our zeal or our power must reach some highest point. We thus close there – this would be the *Satz*-form. Or we return gradually to rest, traversing an opposite path – this is the period with ascending antecedent and descending consequent.

Now there must also exist tone formations that dispense with the closure of a *Satz* or period – for example, every fragment of the preceding formations, without the closing tonic:

Example 2.10

Even the melody in Example 2.4 closes uncertainly and thus insufficiently – at least in the rhythmic domain. We call this sort of tone formation a *Gang*.[8]

---

[8] [Marx:] It already follows from this definition that the *Gang* is not an adequately self-sufficient configuration; it cannot of itself satisfy, as do the *Satz* and period. These latter can in and of themselves be artworks; the *Gang* cannot. Only in Part Two will we familiarize ourselves with its artistic applicability – as a component of larger compositions in which it binds and fuses the various *Sätze* and periods. [Ed.:] Like the word *Satz*, *Gang* will remain untranslated throughout this volume. (See the Introduction, p. 14.)

Review

So far, we have grasped the first concepts of composition and realized them in tones. These were:

1 the *tone succession* in its various *directions* and *types of motion* [i.e. steps and/or leaps];
2 the *initial foundation* of all tone successions, i.e. the *diatonic scale*, and indeed the *major scale*;
3 the distinction between the *moments of rest and motion* in the scale, i.e. the *tonic* on the one hand, and the *remaining tones* on the other;
4 the *rhythmic ordering*, through the addition of which the mere tone succession is raised to a *melody*; with this we were introduced to:
5 determined and manifold *durations* of tones, *metrical division* and *accent*, emphasis of the rhythmic main part from the subordinate parts, etc. Then:
6 the melody strove to gain beginning and end points which were also rhythmically marked and valid, thus closing itself off in all its elements – tonal and rhythmic – and becoming a *Satz*;
7 with this the *manifold variety of rhythmic motion* was introduced, and indeed, as a purposeful variety that serves the sense of the whole; {31}
8 the invented *Satz* then called for its *opposing Satz* and was united with it into a greater whole, the period, in which both *Sätze* stood as *antecedent* and *consequent*;
9 both of the latter revealed their particular characters through the direction of the melody appertaining to each; finally:
10 the essence of a third tone configuration was at least intimated: that of the *Gang*.

With this we have introduced the *three fundamental forms*[9] that underlie all musical configuration: *Satz*, *period*, and *Gang*; and we have apprehended the conditions of their formation.

In the Second Section, entitled "Invention of melodies: the motive," Marx characterizes the motive as a seed [*Keim*] or impulse [*Trieb*]. He

---

[9] [Marx:] Strictly speaking, there are only two fundamental forms, the *Gang* and the *Satz*, since the period is already a combination of one or more *Sätze*. Yet the importance of the period, joining those fundamental forms as the first compound form, makes it advisable to associate it with them. [Ed.:] This sounds less than logical. What Marx means is that the period is important as a primary form, even though it is composed of two (or more) simpler forms.

then analyses previous *Sätze* for their motivic content, identifying the operations of transposition, inversion, augmentation, and diminution. This information is also covered in "Form in music," in Part II of this volume. What must be noted here however, is the pedagogical importance of the fact that Marx introduces motives only *after* introducing the *Satz* and period. This would seem to indicate that he understands the *Satz* – a fully formed musical whole – as the only viable starting point for his compositional method. Wholeness, as always, is paramount for Marx.

The Third Section is entitled "Formation of the *Gang.*" Here Marx more closely defines the *Gang* as a melody without distinct close which arises from the continuation of a motive [Marx, p. 35]. Such a formation must be governed by consistency and logic [*Beharren und Folgerichtigkeit*], a combination that Marx underlines as the first fundamental precept for composition.

SECOND DIVISION: THE TWO-VOICE SATZ

Before resuming actual composition, now with two voices, in Section Three of his Second Division, Marx introduces tonic and dominant harmony. He refers to them as "first harmonic mass" and "second harmonic mass" (tonic and dominant, respectively) and derives them from the overtone series, as shown in Example 2.11. (The number 1 denotes first harmonic mass, number 2, second harmonic mass.)

Example 2.11

Important from the pedagogical point of view is the fact that Marx introduces only as much harmony as is needed to enter into the next stage of composition. Not only does he restrict himself to tonic and dominant, but he does not even present these harmonies initially as triads (note, for example, that the dominant "mass" has no third). He then shows how these two masses can be used to create two-part voicings (i.e. a main voice and an accompanying voice). For a penetrating elucidation of Marx's overall treatment of harmony, see David Kopp, "A comprehensive theory of chromatic mediant relations in mid-nineteenth-century music" (Ph.D. dissertation, Brandeis University, 1995), pp. 73–84.

Section Three: Two-voice composition

{62} After the preparatory exercises in the one-voice *Satz*, we may now proceed more quickly to our goal. We want immediately to form pieces of music in the most complete of the three fundamental forms, namely, the *period*.

Of the period we know that it consists of antecedent and consequent; for now, and for the sake of convenience, we have determined its size to be two times four bars (as in Example 2.9). The close of the one-voice period fell on the tonic. Here, too, the period will close with the tonic, although not with the single tone but with the first harmonic mass, which contains the tonic and which we, for that reason, call the harmony of the tonic or the *tonic harmony*. We place this tonic harmony at the close in such a way (e1, c2) that the tonic, as the most important tone, is given by the main voice and thus sounds most penetratingly. What should precede the tonic?— *Not* another combination of tones from the first mass, but *rather* from the second harmonic mass, which forms the strongest contrast to the first and thus sets it off most prominently. We present this second mass at the end of [our period] with g1 and d2, so that its tones proceed most fleetingly into the tonic closing harmony. Consequently, the close of the period is formed in this way, as the last two harmonies of Example 2.12 show.[10]

How do we close our *antecedent?* — In one-voice composition we closed both the antecedent and consequent with nothing other than the tonic; only the direction of the tone succession distinguished the two parts. Now we are in possession of two harmonic masses, which stand in opposition to each other ... The second mass shares a pair of tone relationships with the first (the octave and especially the fifth – since the octave, fundamentally speaking, provides no essentially different tone[11]); it too can thus help to build a cadence [*Schluss*]. This cadence will suffice for the antecedent, even if it is not as decisive as that of the first mass

---

[10] Marx is actually referring here to an earlier example (his Example 67). Since it shares the features in question with Examples 2.12 and 2.13, I have simply altered his wording to refer to these latter examples.

[11] Marx does not mention the third of the dominant harmony, the leading tone, because he has not yet introduced it as part of the dominant "mass." The reasons behind this omission include both his desire to restrict tonic and dominant to two-voice settings and his derivation of both masses from the overtone series.

(because the {63} tonic is missing and the root, the dominant, is common to both masses and is thus not distinctly characteristic of either of them) ... [12]

Accordingly, our period is formed with the following cadences:

close of the antecedent   close of the consequent

Example 2.12

The last of these, which closes the entire piece, we call a ... *full cadence*; the first, which closes only the first half (the antecedent), we call a *half cadence*. In any event, antecedent and consequent are differentiated more characteristically through these cadences than was the case in one-voice composition.

If we initially fill in the given schema in the simplest way, we have completed our first two-voice composition, which satisfies our immediate needs – but of course does nothing more.

Example 2.13

We have already learned, with simpler material, how to develop more and more again from the scantiest means, by asking what those means offer and what they still lack. Let us thus investigate Example 2.13 from all sides.

First, the new element, harmony: the antecedent stands in the first mass and falls in the second [i.e. opens in the first, closes in the second]; the consequent stands in the second mass and falls in the first. This is very paltry indeed, but since we are as yet new to harmony, it may suffice for now.

Next, the rhythm: it is very impoverished, and we could easily enliven and enrich it, in accordance with what we learned earlier. We could, for example, reshape the antecedent as follows:

[12] [Marx:] Here, too, the relevant reason for this will be revealed only with an understanding of triads.

Example 2.14

With this, however, the main defect of Example 2.13 stands out even more luridly.

{64} It lies in the *tone succession*, which does not even express the normal directionality of antecedent and consequent (p. 43) decisively enough. Since we have come to a provisional understanding of the harmony involved, we now wish to make the antecedent ascend within that harmony, as at a [in Example 2.15].

Example 2.15

Yet the fall from e–g to g–d is too abrupt and necessitates a mediating insertion, as at b. The consequent must now descend, and in a similar fashion; but its predominant second mass offers so little in the way of alternation that we must either repeat one position of it, as in Example 2.16a), or be constrained to enlist the first mass, as in Example 2.16b).

Example 2.16

This consequent lacks only the rhythmic intensification that was attained by the antecedent in Example 2.15b. Here is the entire period, now with the consequent rhythmically intensified at its close (Example 2.17a):

Example 2.17

Note that here, as earlier in Example 2.7, the rhythmic intensification and the deviation from the original version arise out of necessity; even the increased intensification in the consequent was necessary if we were not to declare ourselves satisfied with a tone repetition (b), or with the even less satisfactory manner of Example 2.16.

The progress made from Example 2.14 to Example 2.17 is undeniable; with the latter we have attained a richer tone succession, with a decided directionality and more varied rhythm. Yet the formation is still so simple that, in regard to the melody, only its direction stands out; there is no sharply drawn motive, and the motives in bars 3 and 7 are given no further continuation. Regarding the harmony of these examples, at times we have remained in one mass exclusively for a rather long time and at times we have let both masses alternate with each other. From here on, further progress in invention can offer no difficulty, if only we move forward systematically on our already familiar path. When pursued, every point in the material we have already found leads to new configurations.

If, in Example 2.17, we understand the ascent of the antecedent as staying within the first mass, we can retain this direction in a still more expanded fashion: {65}

Example 2.18

At the same time, the tone succession can be raised to a more varied rhythm and a firmer sense of motivation:

Example 2.19

Or it can be broadened by means of ascent and descent (roving tone succession, p. 38) within the primary direction:

Example 2.20

If we take up the alternation of masses from Example 2.16b, it can serve us as a motive and indeed already in the antecedent; Example 2.17 can be configured as follows, such that a specific motive (a) appears four – or, by counting the diminution in the seventh bar, five – times.

Example 2.21

Several additional examples, in 6/8 time, then follow.

{66} Finally, in that a new series of exercises is to begin at this point,[13] we call attention to the following three considerations.

First: the motive. In one-voice composition, one could speak only of the *tone succession* and *rhythm* of the motive; now one can speak of its *harmonic content* as well – our motives can now either stand only in the first mass or only in the second, or they can unite both masses in diverse ways. With this many-sidedness, however, it is seldom the case that a motive is repeated completely and exactly. For example, the motive a in Example 2.21 retains its rhythmic form four times; the first two times its melody ascends, the last two it goes up and down; in regard to harmony, the first two times it is in the first, then second, mass, the third time in second, first, and second mass, and the fourth time in first, second, and first mass. Nevertheless it remains recognizable. In Example 2.20, now the first mass and now the second mass departs from the rhythm of the motive; at the same time, it is maintained in the other voice.[14]

---

[13] [Marx:] *Third task*: The student is to form a new series in the same steadily progressive manner as the previous *Liedsätze* developed out of and after Example 2.13. All of them must be set and performed in C major, then however (like the earlier exercises) gradually played in the other keys.

[14] It is unclear how this is the case in Example 2.20, as there is no second mass until the end of the phrase.

{67} *Second: the accompaniment.* As mentioned above, we departed from the simple accompaniment of Example 2.13[15] as soon as Example 2.18, in order to lead the second voice upwards more flowingly. The deviations in Examples 2.20 and 2.21 can be left to the reader to elucidate.

Third: From Example 2.13 on, we have formed a series of musical pieces, each of which boasts its own distinctly separate content. Whether or not we find it to be deep and significant, this content can be deemed the idea [*Gedanke*] (the spiritual import) of the piece. Since our compositional efforts remain ever faithful to the motive, each of our pieces contains but one understood idea, even if it undergoes constant elaboration and development ... There are never two different motives ... contained in one of these *Sätze*. Now, a musical piece that holds to only one idea (a unitary [*einig*] content) we call a *Lied* or *Liedsatz*, regardless of whether or not it is meant to be sung. This is in distinction to pieces that contain more than one idea.[16]

---

[15] Again, Marx is here referring to his original Example 67. See note 10 above.

[16] Here at the end of this excerpt, Marx makes an explicit connection to the idea of the spiritual dimension of musical art. He relates the overriding presence of a unitary content, or musical idea, to the spiritual importance of a piece of music. This begins to pave the way for his exaltation of Beethoven, whom Marx has in mind when he says, in an appendix to an earlier edition of vol. I: "Thus the power of all masterworks rests not perchance in the number of individual ideas or traits, but much more in the depth and energy of a single, or of some few, ideas, into which the artist has plunged himself with his entire soul and creative force, and which he has developed lavishly and gloriously in his work." Marx, *Die Lehre*, 2nd edn, vol. 1 (Leipzig: Breitkopf und Härtel, 1841), 399.

PART II

MARX'S *FORMENLEHRE* IN THEORY AND APPLICATION

3

"FORM IN MUSIC"

"Die Form in der Musik," from *Die Wissenschaften
im neunzehnten Jahrhundert*, ed. Dr. J. A. Romberg,
Vol. 2 (Leipzig: Romberg's Verlag, 1856)

Marx wrote the essay "Form in music" for a three-volume collection of essays purporting to present the latest findings of the natural and human sciences to an educated public. Contributors included scholars, artists, and various specialists; the entire collection was assembled and edited by Julius Andreas Romberg, whose own specialty was the history of architecture. Marx's essay was a rare opportunity to discuss musical form outside the context of his compositional method. The result is a presentation of his doctrine of musical form in which he gives full range to the kind of philosophical overtones that he can only suggest within the limits of his treatise. Here is Marx at his most blatantly Idealist: musical form is described in consuming detail as artistic reason coming to know itself through sensuous concretion.[1]

I offer this essay in its complete form; as such it stands as the only unabridged selection in this volume. Here the reader can get an unhindered impression of Marx's writing, for neither I nor Romberg have sacrificed any of his native verbosity, any of the unregulated profusion of rhetorical questions, pseudo-historical asides, bombast, and condescension that no doubt contributed to the impression he invariably made as a brilliant conversationalist. But while Marx will not be remembered as a purveyor of elegantly honed prose, his essay is doubtless a sturdy example of the type of thing one could expect from a nineteenth-century university lecturer who believed he was onto something important. And his enthusiasm is not misplaced: "Form in music" is a major statement on what may well be the most consequential issue in nineteenth-century musical thought.

---

[1] Marx provides a much more succinct overview of his *Formenlehre* in the appendix to the second and later editions of his Beethoven biography.

"Form in music"

Initial view. The concept of form. Evolution of the forms: fundamental forms, artistic forms (song, rondo, sonatina, sonata, figuration, fugue, canon), combined forms (variation, sonata), singular forms [*Einzelformen*] (fantasia, recitative, melodrama). Review.

INITIAL VIEW

{21} One of the most stimulating and initially enigmatic aspects of the nature of music, this most enigmatic of all the arts, is form: the summation of all the manifold configurations in which the content of music appears before our spirit. Is form something fixed, subsisting in and for itself? Does form – any form that has emerged at any time, fittingly or unfittingly – have a right to persist, namely to endure through recurrent use, such that the creative artist must cleave to it, or indeed even subordinate himself to it? Does it in any event carry within itself a useful power for the artist and his listener, a power that compensates for its compulsory imposition? — Or is it merely a thing of tradition, more or less arbitrary, at most a tether and stay for the weak and wayward? Or (to grant a consoling word, in the midst of their hardships, to our practitioners, who live from hand to mouth, and to our genial savages, who are yet again in the business of reinventing the world) could it not in fact be one of those pedantic chimeras of theorists and philosophers, a standpoint now made obsolete? In general: how can one speak of form in art as of something that exists for itself; how can form and content be separated, since the characteristic essence of art rests precisely in its revelation of spiritual content – the Idea – through material embodiment?

These questions, whose circle could easily be broadened, are not the spawn of idle musing. They have an historical warrant in the past and present age, and they will arise again and again in future if one does not succeed in getting to the bottom of the matter, spreading that knowledge [*Erkenntnis*] within the circle of all those who partake in music, and holding fast to it. I say within the circle of all those who partake in music, and not just the artists. For who has yet to realize that it is precisely musicians, who, in their constant oversensitivity and emotional excitation, as well as in the swirling pressures of all their own concerns, are often least inclined and least suited to struggle onward for lucid convictions and then hold fast to them in thought and deed?

{22} Or does it not perhaps speak – to indicate only a few examples – for the mutability of forms, or of artistic inclination, when we observe them change with complete periodicity, when a Bach simply cannot, so to speak, do without the fugue (it pursues him even in his most profound arias), when he perceives the most ambitious of his contemporaries flocking around him in this regard, whereas the same form is indeed known and used by the succeeding age and its masters yet in no way predominates but rather yields pride of place increasingly to the sonata (and its kin, the symphony, quartet, etc.)? — And when, after the mounting establishment and enlargement of sonata form itself, from C. P. E. Bach through Haydn and Mozart up to Beethoven, we see the present age, with Mendelssohn in the lead, inclined toward those miniatures that were earlier known indeed as "bagatelles" and "divertissements" but now wish to take the stage with a completely altered significance, as *Songs without Words* and similar profundities?

Here we observe the alternation of different forms; is not the same form in its own sphere just as mutable? The fugues of Bach and Beethoven – how far from each other they stand in regard to their formation! Simply compare the finales from Beethoven's Sonatas Opp. 106 and 110 with any fugue of Bach. The difference lies not in greater or lesser success, but in the essence of what drives both these artists. The Beethovenian fugues would be untenable in Bach's *Well-tempered Clavier*; no Bach fugue would be tolerable in those sonatas.

Even those formal rights and boundaries within the realm of art are seen to be variable and fluctuating in the course of time. Instrumental music and song necessarily appeared as maximally separable forms; for centuries their union was imaginable only by making the less determinate instrumental music subordinate to song, whose verbal content made it more determinate. Beethoven's Choral Fantasy and Ninth Symphony crossed the dividing line with the most profound artistic warrant, whereas Mendelssohn and Berlioz leapt over it with cheerful abandon.

Indeed, whole species within the realm of art emerge, disappear, and return again. J. J. Rousseau undersigned the *contrat social* of music and spoken word with the melodrama. Benda and others joined in; Mozart spoke very approvingly of the new "genre" and was not disinclined to add to it. It disappeared – only to resurface decades later on the stage (in *Egmont*, *Fidelio*, *Antigone*) and even in the cantata and symphony (Félicien David, Berlioz).

Indeed, it appears that we must welcome this alternation, this variability of forms. The world hungers for the new or, at least, for change in its pleasures. Genius must stride forward, talent strives after it; that which is inwardly unfinished struggles despairingly in the feeling of its emptiness and impotence for some refashioned or even misshapen form, the "circulation of matter" from the inorganic through the organism back to the inorganic belongs {23} every bit as much to the latter days of music as to the younger (and older) discipline of physiology. How could we possibly get on with fixed forms? Forms must change! That is a condition of life. The opposite is stagnation, pseudo-life, death. Form has no right to persist.

So it seems. Indeed, form is not even a reliable support for the weak. Do we not regularly observe around us those wretched mediocrities – who are nowhere so badly off as they are in art – carrying around forms that they picked up here or there, like so many cocoons from which the butterfly, Spirit, has flown? They trouble themselves in vain to fill the fragile husk with new life; thus affixed to the dead, they lose even that feeble remnant of immediacy and individual life that some evil-minded demon poisoned them with in order to lure them into the career of an artist.

Nevertheless, just as we are about to banish form to some distant exile, we find ourselves led back to it at every turn. For it cannot escape us that our greatest masters, in the composition of entire groups of works (e.g. in their fugues, their sonatas and symphonies), not only remained true to themselves but also followed each other closely. The Bach fugues, with all their variety, indicate a master at all points recognizable and true to himself. Taken together, all the Haydn symphonies, or all those of Mozart or of Beethoven, offer themselves – no matter how myriad the content, especially in the case of the last named – as recognizable creations of the same architect. And just as certainly, Mozart's symphonies testify to their origin in those of Haydn, while one need only consider the outward form of Beethoven's symphonies to see that they lean upon those of Mozart; association and succession are every bit as unmistakable here as the progress each master makes beyond his predecessors. The same can be shown in all areas of musical art, e.g. in the forms of opera and its constituent members, in the forms of the cantata and the song – in short, everywhere.

Dare one assume of all, and namely the greatest, of art's masters, that they did not obey an inner necessity that was theirs precisely because they were true artists, but rather that they bent themselves to external motives, to some routine merely handed down, to fashion – and indeed at the cost of everything that fulfills and moves the artist, at the cost of the nature of each one's character, at the cost of the urge for progress, the hunger for fame, even the advantage promised by every mark of distinction?—

These are all considerations from outside, as if from a distance – and already the significance of the question of form is growing. If we approach the matter more closely, if we actually begin to participate in art, then we can no longer fend off such questions. As soon as we get beyond the apathy of mere listening, beyond the most general and superficial perceptions of "This pleases me, and that does not," we cannot but seek a more determinate support in the formation of musical works for our judgement. We distinguish (as far as we are both able and inclined) between the forms that we perceive, be {24} it at times only those that are externally the most discernible; we recognize here the march, there the dance, here the song, there perhaps the fugue (or what we hold to be such), here the recitative, there the fixed song. Only at this point does the mass of all the music that surrounds us separate itself into tendencies and divisions; we compare, we distinguish, measure one against the other, judge one according to the other. Knowledge [*Erkenntnis*] awakens and grows from the perception of form, and only from that perception.

The teacher finds himself even more strictly beholden to form. In every exercise of playing and singing, it is form that first affords an overview of the whole in all its associations and then illuminates the parts themselves. A knowledge of form indicates the alternation of different sections and the return of the same sections; it sets natural goals for musical exercise, goals through which everything is attainable, without wasting one's will and energies on ill-defined material. Only by unlocking the form will the content of the whole become manifest through and through.

Even the outsider knows that determinate exercises – or, rather, determinate forms – are indispensable for the teaching of composition; without them the student would never know what is actually demanded of him, and the teacher would have nothing to express beyond completely indeterminate and indeterminable approval or disapproval. Finally, he who undertakes artistic activity without guidance will not lack sundry stimulation and approbation in our music-saturated atmosphere (and how many have already discovered this!); he bears and feels these things perhaps to a greater degree and more intensely than many a tradesman for whom the inner glow has long since faded in the toil of incessant workdays. And yet! [His artistic effort] will not take shape; it will not come together; it cannot move forward or stand up! It remains in a spasmodic and indeterminate state, directionless and thus formless. Here now is content, something with an inner life; but it cannot find the light of day until it somehow attains a form.

THE CONCEPT OF FORM

What if this last observation were to offer the very key to all the riddles that face us here, the solution of all our contradictions? What if we were able to seize the essence of form, precisely from this standpoint, freeing it from everything arbitrary and erroneous? The solution of the contra-diction and the way to get there – both have perhaps never been so important as they are now, in an age when overheated minds present, as if it were some fiery sun, the dark glow and dismal confusion of their inner and outer distresses both to themselves and to the astonished world, to those they have blinded and bewildered. Clearly: without the warming glow of a heart inflamed with love there is no art. But heat without light, passion without counsel, action without clarity – these can consume, but they can never create. True art is not the product of a cold workshop, but neither is it the reward of demonic incandescence. Art is reason in sensuous appearance; reason is its condition and its content.

{25} We perceived impulses of inner life in such strivings as were left to themselves, yet it was a life without the power to shape itself. In their shapelessness, such impulses remained unsteady, untenable, and incom-prehensible. They were, and are, to the spirit, what cosmic material is to the universe: matter that, in and of itself, is shapeless and indeterminate, and yet becomes everything when it determines itself (regardless from which power) to this and that end, when it splits apart into an opposi-tion, or into many – and thus shapes itself. Gaining shape – form – is nothing other than self-determination, a Being-for-itself apart from the Other.

With this we have gained the *concept of form*, even for art.

Form is not the opposite of content but its determination. Form's opposite is not content in general but rather formlessness – content that is unformed and thus, in its formlessness, undetermined and totally indeterminable. Sounds, vibrations, tones, noises, temporal events: these are themselves not music but rather for music; they are merely the shapeless materials out of which the spirit shapes music. I repeat: for music. That music is not a simple element, recognizable by the physicist or philosopher, but is partly something formed and determined from different elements and their motions and partly a concept deduced from yet other elements – this is not a matter for musicians or for art.

Form in music is thus nothing other than the shaping and hence determination of content that is originally shapeless and undetermined but lies ready in the spirit, eagerly awaiting musical shape, and only then – through shaping, through form – becoming music. The spirit sets its musical content in musical form, sets it firmly and, by so doing, comes to itself, its law, and its consciousness.[2]

Only to the degree that the musical element is shaped and has become form is it music. Moreover, this is not a pronouncement unique to music, but rather the application to music of an entirely general tenet that can be applied just as readily to every other art. With the other arts, however, the question of form has not been so pressing, because the necessity and significance of form is already conditioned and apparent through the object of artistic achievement. The plastic arts (including architecture, horticultural design, and dance) are concerned with the creation or representation of visual forms; the content of poetry is, in all of its works, more or less determined, closed, and knowable, even for those who do not penetrate unto its depths. Those figures of the plastic arts, those human figures and other creatures, those roofs, decks, and supports, those landscape and horticultural objects, have long been familiar to all in their outlines and particularity – that is, in their form. The same goes for the content of all the literary arts, and for linguistics, logic, psychology, and history – whether in the scientific or naturalistic manner. Everyone has already been imbued with such content; it was revealed in a comprehensible form to everyone in advance. Only music appears as that solitary maiden, not of this world, of whom the poet, speaking for most of us, {26} would well have had to say: "one knew not from whence it came." For music stands the farthest from the appear-

---

[2] I have altered the original sentence to make the sense somewhat plainer. The German reads as follows: "In der musikalischen Form setzt der Geist seinen musikalischen Inhalt, setzt ihn fest, kommt in ihm zu sich und seinem Recht und Bewußtsein." The pronoun "ihm" refers to content [*Inhalt*] that has just been shaped and determined, i.e. formed. Thus the spirit is said to come to itself within, or through, this newly formed content. "Die Form in der Musik," 25.

ances and language of wordly life; because of this, life offers only the faintest clue for music and its deeper understanding.

If in music as well as the other arts and, indeed, everywhere, form is that through whose entrance the spirit determines its content and comes to itself, then it follows from this that form is not something external to the spirit, or even imposed from without, and is not something arbitrary, but rather is the unmediated expression of the spirit that has come to itself and, hence, of consciousness. Through form the content of the spirit is determined; through form it is made comprehensible to the intellect; through form alone is the task realizable that reason has set for itself in all the arts and thus also in music.

Above all, then, let us hold fast to this: even in music, form is a necessary thing; it is the sculptor of all works of art, the expression of the rational spirit coming to consciousness and elevating itself to reason – and it is not something arbitrary, not something that imposes itself from without.

Consequently, no one who practices art or who wants only to take up art knowledgeably can dispense with form and pass it by.

Consequently, form must also be comprehended in its truth and its reality, as the product [*Werk*] and expression of the rational spirit striving upward toward reason in art.

Consequently, form – provided that one engages with it – can neither disrupt nor hinder. But when misunderstood, it necessarily does both. Wretched misunderstanding is what disrupts and hinders: not to recognize the rational spirit in form, but to perceive in it the opposite – arbitrary caprice and external compulsion – and hence either to resist form and struggle free from it or to subjugate oneself slavishly to some external precept that would campaign on behalf of "Form," perforce losing the freedom of one's own spirit, that first condition of artistic participation. I cannot think, nor can I feel, through another. It follows that any interest I take in art must emanate from within me, must be born in my own spirit. Consequently, it is not just those newly minted forms I might add to the treasure trove of art that must needs become the property of my spirit; those forms too that have already emerged before me and alongside of me must also become the property of my spirit – and must be born again out of my spirit and my reason, if I would act freely among them. Otherwise they are compulsory, dead and deadening.

This wrongheadedness has sustained no more fitting blow than that of the ingenious Dr. Gumprecht,[3] administered on the occasion of a review (in the *Nationalzeitung*): "the essential attributes of these artificially fabricated overtures and symphonies are a cutting coldness, complete lack of style, and a confused vacillation between trivialities and paradoxes ... Their author holds generally to the traditional form; it stands apart from him as something external, however. His work does not grow organically {27} from the soul, but he instead lays it out mechanically, in accordance with received rules. He thus remains forever without freedom, whether he assumes, against his will, the fetters of his training, or shakes off that burden, in order to bustle about as he pleases. In the latter case, he only exchanges the tyranny of tradition for the much worse despotism of caprice."

EVOLUTION [*ENTWICKLUNG*] OF THE FORMS

Form in art is the sum [*Inbegriff*] of all the formed spiritual content that exists for art. It is divisible, following the evolution of spiritual content, into a corresponding *series of forms*. There must be just as many forms as exist developmental stages [*Entwicklungen*] of spiritual content, just as many as exist the possibilities and need of the spirit to set itself (its content *per se* or its artistic content), to bring itself to consciousness.

The evolution of this series of forms has been the historical task of all artists faithful to their calling. Each artist has been able to make already established forms his own; each has been able to add new forms to these. Both possibilities must be openly recognized by all living artists and by those to come, for as long as there remains a spiritual impetus that demands concretion through music.

For this reason, the series of forms may be deemed *infinite*; at least no one can point to an end, or cut-off point, of the series, as long as music maintains its place in the realm of human affairs — that is, forever. For that which the human spirit has begotten in accordance with the necessity of its essence is created forever, even if it does not always remain in the same esteem, i.e. court the same urgency, or stay forever untransformed.

An enumeration of the forms that have appeared up to now might even have some worth as historical information. Yet, this worth would be belittled, since our count — over and against the enduring possibility

---

[3] Dr. Otto Gumprecht (1823–1900), a music critic who wrote several books on Wagner.

of fresh progress – would be complete for today only and not for tomorrow. Such external compilation would have, however, no more scientific significance than that external grasping, by an erring artistic confederacy, of forms in which the spirit has not come alive. Ever since we have recognized form not as something external but as the creation and expression of artistic reason itself, this can no longer suffice.

If form is at all a thing of reason, then each particular form must also be created out of reason – or be judged and then discarded by reason as an untenable error. Such a judgement is not entrusted to this or that judge, no matter who appointed him, nor to the past, the present, or the future, but rather to reason, singular and eternal – though comprehended in its eternal evolution. This also invalidates (by the by) that recently circulated subterfuge with which minds more heated than brilliant would like to disarm the judgement of {28} their contemporaries, namely, that an entire generation of contemporaries has often been wrong before, and that the final decision belongs only to the future (which future?). The future, too, has often erred, e.g. all those centuries that held Vergil, the imitator, in higher esteem than Homer. Let us trust only reason! And if reason were to be awakened in but a single contemporary, he alone would then have the power for, and over, the rest.

If reason is both judge and creator of forms, then it is incumbent upon reason to pass judgement not only on newly appearing forms but also on the preservation of existing forms or their transformation, their transition into other forms, or even their demise. Bach's preludes close in the main key, and are thus self-sufficient – one must have realized that in so doing they relinquish the strongest possible connection to the following main movement; these and other such introductory movements were henceforth brought to a less autonomous close. The suites of Händel and Bach string together a series of different movements (up to eleven) that are all in the same key and mostly in the same mode; in sonatas, symphonies, etc., the variety of content is given profile through changes of key. The form of the suite thus underwent a transition into that of the sonata or, if you will, disappeared in the wake of the sonata.

Through the series of all the forms that have been, that live still, and that are to come, we thus see artistic reason alone hold sway as creator and judge. Caprice, contemporary tastes and fashions, or whatever other external determinations one can name – these matter not a whit; their influence can come to the fore only as untenable error in individual cases.

With this certainty, the series of forms appears to much greater advantage than is the case with that external enumeration to which things seemed to be tending earlier on. The system of forms thus makes its appearance as applied logic, as it were; a history of forms (the like of which has not yet been written and must remain unwritten for some time yet) would narrate the evolution of spirit in music.

If we finally enter into the evolution of the various forms, we find we must distinguish *fundamental forms*, which serve as the precondition and foundation for all formal configurations in music; *artistic forms* or genre forms, which are mutually valid for certain general directions of musical life, and to which may be added *combined forms*, larger wholes consisting of individual autonomous movements; and *singular* forms, which guarantee the particular (let us say subjective) right and need of every individual configuration within the world of artistic forms. Common to all or many, the need for, and the right to, subjectivity stand equally under the aegis of reason.

The *influence of the material*, in which the spirit embodies itself artistically, runs through all the classes of form (it is especially prominent in the first and second classes).[4] For the material, too, is not seized upon arbitrarily and insignificantly; on the contrary, the spirit finds and seizes the appropriate material for each of its revelations. It is one spirit that reveals itself now in tones, {29} and now in words or visible shapes, and that allows now music, and now literary or plastic art, to spring forth, tracing for itself three closely related and yet essentially distinct directions. It is one and the same spirit, turned to music, that reveals itself now in tones, now in rhythms, now in instruments, now in song, in closely related and yet essentially distinct emanations.

Finally, the *alliance of music with the other arts and with life* appears as the source for forms that are to be distinguished as new. Here the spirit does not rule entirely and freely within the element of music; rather this element is one of the conditioning factors of the spirit's ability to rule, no matter whether it be a leading or a subordinate one.

Let us now peruse the series of forms. The mandate of these pages forbids us to present everything here. We are duty bound to admit only so much as aids the thinking reader, even were he not a musician, to be able to find secure bearings in the wide world of musical form and

---

[4] By first and second classes of forms, Marx may be referring to the fundamental forms and the artistic forms, the first two classes of forms described above.

recognize the sway of reason throughout. Further treatment is taken up in the author's treatise on composition.

Demonstration with successions of tones

The first necessity is this: that the spirit, in order to reveal itself in music, seizes upon musical material.

Such a thing is not yet decided with a single tone, or chord, etc. In opposition to the single sound or tone stands silence, to which that tone is again remanded; here the spirit touches musical material but immediately denies it once again.

Only the succession of two or more tones (chords, rhythmic events, etc.) shows the spirit persisting in the musical element. I have systematically referred to the linking of two or more tones (or other unities within the musical element) as a *motive*. I would have preferred the name *germ* or *impulse* if the expression "motive" were not already thoroughly at home in artistic and mundane discourse, and if it did not appear advantageous to confer upon this expression, lost as it is in slippery vagueness (it designates a melody, a fragment of melody, a phrase built out of melody and harmony – anything one wants), a firmly determined and useful, indeed indispensable, significance.

The motive is the primal configuration [*Urgestalt*] of everything musical, just as the germinal vesicle, that membranous sac filled with some fluid element (or perhaps with solid bodies), is the primal configuration of everything organic – the true primal plant or primal animal. The motive, this conjunction of two tones or some other unities, simply *is*. At first it is for itself, without further relation, as yet a thing incomplete and unsettled; this is already evident in the indefinite quality of its content and its extent. I put forth the tones c2–d2 as a motive – why not others; why not more? This is indeed {30} only a beginning, a germ, one that can grow further or perhaps will thrive no longer. Even in this last case it is something other than the single tone. In that it contains more than a singularity, it shows a persistence and propagation in the musical element, whether it leads to different singularities or to related versions of the same singularity. It thus already boasts not just material content but also spiritual content.

The spirit has now engaged itself in this particular motive and in no other. The spirit must then have found some relation to it; either no other motive presented itself to the spirit – the relation of limitation, of impoverishment – or it showed itself to be the most suitable among other available motives – the relation of inclination or attraction. In both cases the spirit is free to let it go again and take up other motives in the alternation of attractive force or inclination, or to retreat entirely from this particular musical field. The spirit can also persist in the selected motive, however; it can simply repeat it: c2–d2, c2–d2; or repeat it in other circumstances, e.g. those of transposition: c2–d2, d2–e2; or of direction, or of transposition and direction: c1–d1, d1–c1, ... c1–d1, e1–d1, etc.

If we could best ascribe the act of taking up a motive to inclination, then with its repetition – and even more strongly with repetition in varied circumstances – the intellect comes into play. For even in the case of mere persistence, the spirit already shows itself aware of its initial impulse and firmly secure in will; it is at one with itself and has determined itself. In that it now moves that which was originally taken up further along, bringing it into other circumstances without losing it, it makes itself master of the motive and, in its impulse to adhere to the motive, frees itself of those circumstances, and in fact rules them as well. Here already is actual artistic formation [*Kunstgebilde*], in which the spirit not only announces itself, as in the primal configuration (the motive), but acts creatively. I have felt constrained to designate this species of formation as a *Gang*, for the essential thing is the further motion of the motive through displacement into other circumstances; this stands out most noticeably in the process of leading through various key centers.

The *Gang* is the *first fundamental form* in music.

Where does the end of a *Gang*, of any *Gang*, occur? Nowhere. It stops somewhere or other, as everything must at some point stop, because strength, time, or desire expires, or because some external goal has been reached. There exists no reason within the *Gang* itself to come to a close. In the following series: c1–d1, d1–e1, e1–f1 ... , instead of breaking off at e1–f1 I could just as easily continue through f1–g1 and go still further.

In the *Gang* itself no satisfaction can be found; rather the very act of moving forth is a search for satisfaction. {31} Only the attaining of some goal that I set for myself or appropriate can satisfy me, in that it elevates my will to a state of consummation.

Within the succession of tones only one tone can be the goal, and it could be any – no matter for what reasons it is selected. If we began our first motive with the tone c, then this tone appears provisionally as the one that is at first suitable for us or that is agreeable to us (no matter why). Now, however, if this our preferred tone is left behind, abandoned, in our original motive or in this succession to that motive: c2–d2, ... c2–b1, then we have lost the object of our satisfaction. Consequently we must win back this satisfaction by returning to its object: c2–d2–c2, ... c2–b1–c2.

Here, in the smallest space and with the scantiest of means, we see that a new and higher formation has arisen. This progress does not lie in the increase of tones, from two to three; we could have presented motives of three and more tones earlier, e.g. c–d–e, ... c–d–e–f–g, without any essential progress. The decisive thing is rather that one of the tones has achieved precedence, winning the preference of our spirit, such that we fix it as the goal of our striving, that we are for that reason induced to return to it, to end with it, because we are finished and satisfied with it.

With this, a *judgement* has been made: a series of tones has been closed off for internal reasons and thus is fixed. A thought that is closed in and of itself is called a *Satz*. Its conclusion is its characteristic feature. The *Gang*, too, must stop sometime and somewhere, like everything; but it takes an ending only for external reasons – it does not close. The *Satz* closes for internal reasons.

The *Satz* is the second fundamental form in music.

Everything that is formed [*gebildet*] in music is either *Gang* or *Satz*, or a compound of both. There is no third fundamental form. If, in my compositional method, I associated the period with the fundamental forms, it was only for reasons of method, in order to keep this important and ubiquitously hard-working form constantly before the student's eyes from the very beginning. It is clear (I pointed it out even there) that the period is only the joining of two or more *Sätze* and is thus not a fundamental form.[5]

We initially represented the choice of a goal tone as an arbitrary choice, as the expression of some chance inclination or resolution. With this the subjective right of every artisan [*Bildner*] finds its voice.

A higher, objective determination of a goal tone becomes possible when necessarily coherent and self-sufficient musical regions are formed from the essence of the realm of music, regions that have as a

---

[5] See Part I, p. 45.

basis one of their constituent tones acting as a fundamental tone. {32} The major mode is one such musical region, built on some degree or other, e.g. on c1: c1 d1 e1 f1 g1 a1 b1 ... and c2. This series of tones is anything but arbitrarily assembled or based simply on tradition (of about two and a half millennia, by the way). It contains (after originally having remained stalled with five scale degrees) the seven scale degrees that appeared initially in the development of the tonal system (f c g d a e b), now arranged in a more suitable succession and having the tone c as foundation or "preferred tone," as *tonic*. Even the original pentatonic series of the Orient: f c g d a, or, practically ordered, f g a ... c d ..., shows a tonic, indeed as its actual starting tone.

A recognition of the significance of the tonic was not necessary for the continued use of both of these successions of tones; the ancient Orientals, Greeks, Romans and Gaels did not always conclude their tunes on the tonic – far from it! They often preferred to break off on some other tone: the unboundedness that had become dear to them in their high plains, in the unlimited mirror of the sea, and in their relent-less army campaigns made itself felt in their song by dint of the subjec-tive right founded in their circumstances and moods, and in accordance with the unevolved state of their musical consciousness.[6] We too can forgo a conclusion on the tonic for subjective reasons.

In the meantime, the tonic must be recognized, in accordance with reason, as the goal tone and generally satisfying concluding tone; all remaining tones are but a striving, a motion through tones, to the tonic, whether we start out from some other tone or from the tonic itself. The tonic is thus the normative close for us and for that reason has come to prevail with incalculable preponderance, against which other endings of a musical whole, as isolated exceptions, are hardly worth considering.

With this the essence of the *Satz* is elevated from the lowly standpoint of arbitrary formation to the realm of inner necessity, i.e. rationality.

In addition, it is well known that not only can the normal tonal system of the major mode be represented on each of the twelve half steps, thereby yielding the twelve major keys, but that alongside this a minor mode exists as well, presentable in twelve minor keys, and that the

---

[6] This type of historical account, so overtly biased toward the eventuality of tonal music, is not at all unusual in nineteenth- and even twentieth-century discussions of musical materiality among the ancients.

middle ages formed and bequeathed to us the church modes or so-called Greek modes, successions which diverge more or less from both the major and minor modes. All of these are indeed so many musical realms, which stand open to the same fundamental features of *Satz* construction. {33} The question of the suitability of the chromatic scale for the same (or rather, why it is not so suited) does not belong here.

Demonstration in the realm of harmony

We have recognized tonic and the series of remaining tones as an opposition, as goal and the motion to the goal. This opposition is repeated and fulfilled in harmony. Over and against the harmony of the tonic (the tonic triad) stand all the remaining harmonies, the former as goal and consummation, the latter as motion to the goal. The carrier and representative of harmonic motion, however, is the *dominant chord*,[7] by dint of its express lack of sufficiency and its inclination toward the tonic harmony.

This is represented concretely in the following two examples: 1) under the scale stretching and leading from tonic to tonic, as well as 2) under the scale arranged around the tonic, its goal and center of gravity:

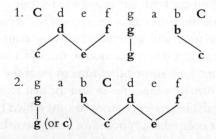

The dominant chord (with or without added ninth, which extends it to a ninth chord without essentially altering its nature) marks the closest relation to the scale of its key center, in that it can be reproduced in no other. At the same time, it does not contain within itself the goal and resting point of the scale, the tonic. This inner contradiction compels it to seek rest and resolution outside itself, namely in the tonic and its harmony.

With this we have gained a new axiom: the close of a *Satz* happens

---

[7] Here Marx means the dominant seventh chord, which he sees as the fundamental form of the dominant.

harmonically through the motion (the technical expression is *resolution*) of the dominant or ninth chord to the tonic with its harmony. We must leave aside any discussion of exceptions and their causes.

Demonstration in rhythm

The spirit lingers longest with that which is most important to it, likewise bringing its strongest will [*Wollen*] to bear upon the principal matter. Lingering and emphasis, meter [*Zeitmaß*] and accent, are the elements of rhythm.

Emphasis and lingering are fitting for the closure of the *Satz* on the tonic and its harmony, the goal and end of the whole. The main beat within the prevailing meter must be conceded to this goal point.

ARTISTIC FORMS [*KUNSTFORMEN*]

Let it first be said that this designation is not strictly suitable, and that the expression "compound forms" would be more systematic. For a mere *Satz* can be a complete artistic work, since it carries within itself closure and sufficiency, as can be seen, *inter alia*, in the chorale "Wahrlich, {34} dieser ist Gottes Sohn gewesen" in Bach's St. Matthew Passion. In such a case, then, a fundamental form must be recognized as an artistic form. Yet the scales are decisively tipped against such infrequent exceptions by common sense and traditional parlance.

Artistic forms are the forms of complete art works. Apart from the few cases in which the single *Satz* is itself the form of an art work, artistic forms are joined together out of *Sätze* and *Gänge*.

In accordance with what law does the formation of artistic forms ensue?

With that same steadily progressing law that we designated above as the product of logic, when applied to music.

Before going any further, let us summarize what we have acquired so far.

We have a major and minor mode, each presentable in twelve keys, each key acting as the essence of a group of tones that intrinsically belong together, with the tonic of each key acting as that key's main tone and as the goal that provides sufficient gratification. We have harmonies, namely the tonic triad and the dominant chord, antitheses that represent goal and motion. We have the temporal and accentual emphases of rhythm. We have threefold closure for the *Satz*: in the scale, the harmony, and the rhythm. By the by, we mentioned the chromatic scale; though it is not, like the key centers, suited to serve as the foundation of artistic formations, as do the key centers, it can yet participate in such formations.

From all these means we eventually formed the *Satz*.

It is possible for such *Satz* formation to happen without logical consequence [*Folgerichtigkeit*], for us to hang one unrelated motive arbitrarily onto another and in the end lend the motley result, by means of a correct cadence, the appearance of coherence. Yet here the spirit has not been engaged; because it lets one motive drop alongside another, it has not held to that which it willed and with which it began.

It is artistic – because in accordance with reason – to adhere to what has been begun, that is, to adhere to the motive until it has been adequately expressed, until we have progressed further, with and through the motive, and earned the right and possibility of closure. My compositional method has more to say about this. The artistically correct *Satz* must therefore be unified and coherent in respect to content and form.

Here we enter into the artistic forms. The first to appear are those that are presentable completely through the means we have discussed to this point, namely through a melody alone (a rhythmicized succession of tones) or through melody supported by harmony. The harmony is carried out by one or more series of tones (voices) but remains, however configured, in a subordinate relation throughout to the melody, as subsidiary matter to the principal matter; it is called accompaniment.

We may sum up the complete series of artistic forms structured in this way (obviously a completely different manner of structuring is also possible) as {35}

Homophony

Here it is as if everything belongs to the melody, the *principal voice*, as if all the voices count as the same, as one voice.

The artistically correct *Satz*, namely one that is unified in construction, grounds the first of the homophonic forms, which we call:

Song form [Liedform], *or* Liedsatz

It goes without saying that one can build many such *Sätze*, that one can let two or more of these follow each other temporally, linking them to each other. Such succeeding *Sätze* could even have a certain relation to their predecessors, in that they appear in the same or in a nearby (*closely related*) key, and also share the same meter and tempo [*Bewegung*]. Even so, these kinds of relations are very superficial; the content of the various *Sätze* can be alien and incoherent when juxtaposed. Each *Satz* can then count as a *Liedsatz*, but their succession cannot count as a unified whole. This latter requires *unity of content* among everything that would together form a whole, as in the single artistically correct *Satz*.

Yet every motive may be deemed to be of infinite application. I can take the motive c–d and repeat it in the same position as often as I like; I can transpose it to any other, thus changing it; I can present it in the opposite direction (*inversion*): d–c; I can extend it or compress it: c–e, ... c–d♭; I can alter its rhythm or its accompaniment; and I can do all these things in varied manners, successions, and mixtures. Thus it becomes evident that no *Satz* actually exhausts its content – although it may work its content sufficiently enough for a specific artistic purpose, as in the above case.[8]

From this it follows that every *Satz* is one-sided, that one can glean other, even opposed, sides from its content, giving the *Satz* a consequent [*Nachsatz*] or an opposing phrase [*Gegensatz*]. These two (or more) phrases belong to each other, in accordance with their related content, and can form an internally unified whole; such a whole is called a *period*.

The period is the first compound form and the second song form after the *Satz*. It consists primarily of two internally unified *Sätze*, which are called antecedent [*Vordersatz*] and consequent [*Nachsatz*] – or it can consist of more: two antecedents and a consequent, an antecedent and two consequents, two antecedents and two consequents, etc. The non-musician can visualize these possible developments with the following abstract formulas; they have the same comprehensibility and make the same claim:

if A, then (possibly) C
if A and B, then C
if A, then C and D
if A and B, then C and D.

{36} But the unity of the period must also be formally prominent. The opposite occurs when its first *Satz* closes with complete gratification, as we determined above with the fundamental form of the *Satz*. For after total gratification there is no need for anything further; continuation is

---

[8] We may assume that Marx is referring to the example from Bach's St. Matthew Passion, on p. 71.

not expected and is not perceived as appropriate. If one desires to avoid this, one must take up still other forms of closure than that completely satisfying manner of closing peculiar to the fundamental form, closures that indeed satisfy to a certain, provisional, extent but not totally, not once and for all.

Our initial manner of closure brings motion to rest and satisfies, in that it leads that motion to the goal tone of the key center from which the *Satz* took its essential content. At the same time, this goal tone was to have been the primary tone rhythmically; it was to have been accompanied by its own harmony (if harmony there were), the tonic triad. Let us add that in this latter case the following is necessary for complete gratification: the two harmonies which form the close, dominant chord and tonic triad, must appear in the firmest manner (on their fundamental tones), and the last chord must have the most important tone (the tonic) in both of its most prominent voices (the uppermost and lowest voices).

This manner of closure is called a *full cadence*; it forms and marks the close of a totality. It is called a *perfect* full cadence when it appears in the form just described, that which most satisfies.

From this one can now gather that there yet exists a series of less satisfying closures.

To begin with, the full cadence itself can appear in a less satisfying form, as an *imperfect* full cadence.

Or a full cadence can be formed but in a different key. The *Satz* is thus led to a goal but not to its original goal; it has ventured out of its tonal homeland into a foreign land and may indeed settle there – but it will never rid itself of its recollection of the homeland and the feeling of being a foreigner. Only in the homeland – that is, through renewed motion, return, and settlement in the homeland (through a final full cadence) – can complete satisfaction be attained.

What if one could achieve the same or similar effect but stay within the main key? Then the need for further progress would be satisfied along with an enhanced feeling of unity. We find such an effect vouchsafed in the form of the *half cadence*.

For reasons which cannot be discussed here, modulation (the motion from one key into another) is directed originally and in most cases to the key of the dominant; one regularly proceeds, for example, from C major to G major. Here one finds g–b–d to be the tonic triad, the same triad contained in the foundation of the dominant chord of C major. Now the full cadence goes from dominant to tonic, i.e. – in terms of the fundamental tones – from G (dom.) to C (ton.), {37} and the dominant chord indeed stands on G. Technically speaking, this is how the *Satz* that is complete in and of itself must close, and so too the period, i.e. its last member, its consequent – assuming that full gratification is intended. The consequent is the opposing phrase (the opposite) to the antecedent, and vice versa. It follows that the antecedent's form of closure must be the opposite of that of the consequent; it must take the opposite path from C (ton.) to G (dom.) – with the only difference that it must refrain from using the dominant chord[9] (which would immediately hurry back to C) and be content with the triad on the dominant. This is the normative half cadence. Another type arises only as an expedient in certain cases; it is discussed in my compositional method.

In these cadences the artistic spirit has thus created, thoroughly in accordance with reason, the means by which the antecedent and consequent phrases (one or more) of the period can be led to endings in such a way that each party is rounded off self-sufficiently with the degree of gratification appropriate to it, while complete gratification is attained only with the final closure, thus stamping the whole as a coherent totality.

Two- and three-part song form

The normative half cadence of the antecedent phrase remains within the main key; through this means the *Satz* attains firmer unity. Yet another outcome is also possible; instead of this half cadence, a full cadence in another key may occur.

This division is obviously stronger, and one will not likely rush to use it as readily as the less encumbered half cadence; one will find occasion and space for it only when one has sufficiently exploited the main keynote [*Hauptton*].

Then what previously was called antecedent and consequent now elevates itself to a greater abundance and significance, as well as to a more decisive division: the antecedent becomes the *First Part*, the consequent the *Second Part*, of a larger whole; each part – or one only – can again be divided into antecedent and consequent, i.e., can assume periodic form.

What content will these two parts have? The possibility that two *Sätze* of differing content can follow each other and even be superfi-

---

[9] The dominant seventh chord (see note 7).

cially connected to each other has already been recognized above; this same possibility exists for the two parts of a *Liedsatz*. Yet coherence and unity obviously grow when both share the same basic content [*Grundgehalt*]. This common content naturally appears initially in the first part, hence as it originally appeared to the artisan [*Bildner*].[10] In the second part the content may be intensified or equipped with some new power to attract: the echo of the initial formation will always linger with continued effect in the creative spirit; in the end, the second part will gladly return to the beginning or to a principal moment of the first part.

Indeed, if the second part has established itself and spread out to such an extent {38} that there is no space before its close to come back to the first part, then it will build a cadence for itself of such a nature that the repetition of the entire first part can then follow. This repetition admits of variation, being compelled to redirect its cadence into the main key if the first part closed in another key; it appears as the third part.

The *Satz* has engendered the period; the period has extended itself into two separate parts; binary form has grown to ternary form – the unity of content and configuration is the crowning task throughout.

Combination *of* Liedsätze

Music can advance further. But for its more comprehensive tasks, it has richer and more mobile forms than the *Liedsatz*. Within the song form there are only two remaining stages: an energetic stage and another more arbitrary stage.

One can follow and contrast a two- or three-part *Liedsatz* with another one of divergent content. There then remains (as before with the second part) a memory of and desire for the first *Liedsatz*, which invites its repetition. This first *Satz* is called the main *Satz* [*Hauptsatz*], the other is called the trio (and is more mild, because the original impulse is expended on the main *Satz* and the power to close belongs to it by right). Main *Satz*, trio, and repetition of main *Satz* again present a ternary nature, only in a higher stage of development. Our examples include marches and polonaises, the minuets and scherzi of our sonatas, etc.

One can string together (as Strauss and Lanner did with especial

---

[10] Marx is dubiously associating temporal priority within the composition with compositional priority.

luster in their waltz cycles) any number of *Liedsätze* with a superficially unifying plan of modulation that leads from one to the other, perhaps returning ultimately to the beginning, or, then again, perhaps not. Here the content, extent, and arrangement is arbitrary and, for that reason, the unity less energetic.

Returning once more to the ternary *Liedsatz*, we see that with its richer development it excites the need for a more powerful closure. How is this demand to be met? By staying longer with the final chords, by repeating them, or by a harmonic progression [*Modulation*][11] that drives forth to them. This leads to extended *closing formulas* that can indeed build their own particular melodies (not derived from the primary content) and are then called *closing Sätze*. They serve, then, as a more satiating closure of the main *Satz* – namely, of the first part and its repetition as third part, each time in the key of the conclusion. If they appear merely at the end of the whole, or with particular prolixity (perhaps with reference to the primary content), then they are said to form an *appendix* or *coda*. They are found most reliably and recognizably at the end of the first and third parts in the first, allegro, movement of sonatas; in these movements they enter when the primary content, now in the closing key, turns to its conclusion.

It is evident that in the closing *Sätze* the unity of content we treated as a characteristic feature of the song form is no longer {39} (or not necessarily) present. And it is just as evident that the closing *Satz* reveals itself as something incidental, added only for a secondary purpose (cadential strengthening cannot be absolutely necessary to the content).

Even so, in the closing *Satz*, as in the linking together of various *Liedsätze* to a larger whole, the limits of the song form can be felt – as well as its lack of determinacy. This lack of determinacy is not an error lying perhaps in the matter itself or in its presentation. It is rather a fitting and very promising expression of spiritual freedom in art, which can satisfy itself in accordance with its then existing needs as well within a given form as by stepping beyond its bounds, and satisfying itself elsewhere.

Every form is a restraint, a fetter for the spirit that has come to belong to it. With every succeeding form, the spirit is released into a new perspective. The spirit is free only when it possesses all the forms, as well as

---

[11] Marx often uses the word *Modulation* to denote any harmonic progression. See note 17 below, on p. 133.

the complete power to build them – and, in requisite cases, to build new ones. Every form is an expression of formative reason, which finds its complete justification only in the sum [*Inbegriff*] of all forms.[12]

The rondo forms

While discussing the systematic union of two different *Liedsätze*, we have called the first of these the main *Satz*. Let us again proceed from such a main *Satz*. Say that I have fixed it and closed it off – and yet I still don't feel satisfied; something within still feels in motion. What is moving me? — I myself do not recognize it clearly; I only feel myself urged ahead, farther, I know not where. If I knew it, I would have a determined object in front of me as the goal of this urge. Musically, this goal would thus take on that fundamental form that is firmly closed in and of itself, the *Satzform*, or else one of the song forms derived from it. But since this is not the case, it brings on that fundamental form that is not firmly closed off in and of itself, but that only expresses motion: the *Gang*.

A main *Satz* and a *Gang* leading from the main *Satz* are the components of the *first rondo form*. But the *Gang*, which finds no gratification nor any ending within itself, also cannot function as the close of a larger whole. The main *Satz* must return and close, because it is the main *Satz* (like the first part in the song forms) – and because presumably we have no other *Satz*.

From whence do we derive the *Gang*? Either we build it from arbitrarily grasped foreign motives – here there is no inner connection with the main *Satz*, and only its return can finally set things right – or we create the material for the *Gang* out of the main *Satz* itself, in that we link up with its content and use it to move forward from its conclusion, as if to suspend that conclusion, perhaps already having excited the urge for further motion before the conclusion. Here the *Gang* appears as *further motion from the main Satz* and is in complete unity of content with it. In either case the *Gang* leads to a point {40} (usually the dominant of the main tonic) from which the return of the main *Satz* may comfortably proceed.

The urge to advance was present in the first rondo form but found no

---

[12] Here, *in nuce*, is Marx's view of the motivation for his derivation of forms. Artistic reason, in conjunction with the spirit's demand for freedom, drives and controls the evolution of form.

determinate object. Now it is time to find one. Yet which form could possibly step forth here? Not the *Gang* (for it is the opposite of determinacy) but the *Satz*, or one of the song forms derived from it. This new *Satz* steps to the side of the main *Satz*; it is not the principal matter (as little as is the trio in the song forms) but subordinate matter. It is thus called the subordinate *Satz*, or *subsidiary Satz* [*Seitensatz*]. But precisely because it is only subordinate matter, and not the main idea, it cannot offer final gratification; we must return to the main *Satz*, in order to find therein full gratification and a unified rounding off of the whole.

This return of the main *Satz* can happen without mediation, immediately after the close of the subsidiary *Satz*; we then have before us a *Liedsatz* with Trio, as has already been designated above. Or we can impel ourselves out of the subsidiary *Satz* by attaching a *Gang* to it and then returning to the main *Satz* in this manner, as in the first rondo form.

This is the *second rondo form*, whose essential content can be visualized as follows:

$$MS - SS - G \curvearrowright MS$$
(main *Satz*, subsidiary *Satz*, transition point for the
return [*Gangpunkt der Umkehr*], main *Satz*)

This form outdoes the song form with Trio through its flowing coherence, and it points toward those configurations that make unlimited expansions of the song form (as mentioned above) unnecessary and unadvisable.

It is possible for the subsidiary *Satz* to appear in the same tonal region as the main *Satz*. But because it wants to be an Other to the main *Satz*, it is more fitting for it to choose another key or at least to change its mode. In the first case, keys that stand in closer proximity (*relation*) to the main key take precedence over those that are more distant; these are the keys of the dominant, subdominant, parallels, and mediants – concerning which my compositional method provides information. Yet even more distant relationships can establish themselves.

Since one can fashion innumerable *Sätze*, it is also possible to form more than one subsidiary *Satz* in the rondo – two, for example, and each provided with its own key. The above diagram represents a closed rondo with one subsidiary *Satz*. What if there were a need for further progress after its close? Then a second subsidiary *Satz* in a new key would arise; it too would not be able to offer final satisfaction and would have to

lead back, through a new *Gang*, to another repetition of the main *Satz*.
This is the *third rondo form*, portrayed in the following diagram:

$$MS - SS1 - G \frown MS - SS2 - G \frown MS$$

In this form the first subsidiary *Satz* appears as a first attempt to come
away from the main *Satz*, the second subsidiary *Satz* as a second attempt; only with this latter {41} is the dissatisfaction with the main *Satz*
repeated, thus coming to the fore more sharply. From this one may
conclude that the first subsidiary *Satz*, in accordance with reason, must
be of lighter tenor, passing by more fleetingly, while the second subsidiary *Satz* must be weightier and more developed, as well as more firmly
rounded off.[13] The same applies to both *Gänge*.

A glance at the diagram already shows that the thrice repeated main
Satz prevails decisively; however, the first (and more lightly fashioned)
of the subsidiary *Sätze* runs the risk of being forgotten in all the ensuing
music, whereas the second subsidiary *Satz*, more firmly fixed and the last
to appear, has a more lasting effect. One can be satisfied with this (as is
often the case), or one can take a more lasting interest in the first subsidiary *Satz*.

If so, one must return to it and repeat it like the main *Satz* – and
indeed not [immediately] before or after the second subsidiary *Satz*
(because these foreign sections would be all too oppressive in close juxtaposition) but after the last repetition of the main *Satz*.

This results in the *fourth rondo form*, whose course and content is
shown in the following diagram:

$$MS - SS1 - G \frown MS - SS2 - G \frown MS - SS1$$

If it closes with the first subsidiary *Satz*, then this latter must above all
leave its earlier key for the main tonic. But how will it – secondary idea
of the lightest tenor and framework! – guarantee final gratification? One
will require an *appendix* (as was already mentioned with the song form),
taken from the main *Satz* or one of the other sections [*Partien*] of the
rondo. Even the earlier forms, indeed all artistic forms, grant final confirmation by means of an appendix.

But is the main *Satz* of a rondo always in fact worthy of three appear-

[13] What Marx seems to be implying here is that the first subsidiary *Satz*, as an initial, and ultimately unsuccessful, attempt to come away from the main *Satz*, must needs be of a lighter and
less consequential character. Were it more consequential there would presumably remain no
need for a second attempt.

ances? Or indeed four appearances, when an appendix fashioned out of it is included?—

It can be omitted from the middle of the form. But then the first subsidiary *Satz* rushes without relief to the second! We must create such relief, by closing off the whole first section [*Partie*]. The *Gang* cannot of itself close satisfactorily; we provide it with a concluding *Satz*, a *closing Satz* (known already from the song forms) and may now proceed, having collected ourselves, to the second subsidiary *Satz*. The closing *Satz* reappears, reasonably enough, in the last prevailing tonal region, the key of the first subsidiary *Satz*. Naturally we employ its closing power for the final close as well, after the repetition of the (first) subsidiary *Satz*; it goes without saying that it now appears, along with that subsidiary *Satz*, in the main key.

If we designate the closing *Satz* with CS, we now see the diagram for the newly arisen *fifth rondo form*:

$$\text{MS SS1 G CS} - \text{SS2 G} \frown - \text{MS SS1 G CS}$$

This again shows a clearly delineated ternary structure; this structure and several of the most probable arrangements of keys are manifest in the following table: {42}

I.				II.			III.			
MS	SS1	G	CS	– SS2	G	⌒ –	MS	SS1	G	CS
C maj.	G maj.		G maj.	C min.			C maj.	C maj.		C maj.
				E min.						
				E♭ maj.						
A min.	C maj.		C maj.	F maj.			A min.	A min.		A min.
				F min.				(A maj.)		(A maj.)
				A♭ maj.						

My compositional method provides a more detailed account of modulation.

If we survey all the rondo forms together, we see that they have decisively surpassed the loose organization of a mere song-chain (a succession of *Liedsätze* linked together) and have attained a solid coherence among their parts. At the same time, however, we cannot fail to recognize a certain lightness (if not to say looseness) in their character. They allow the main *Satz* to fall away, only in order to bring it back again, then perhaps to abandon it once more and once more bring it back. They give up the first and the second subsidiary *Satz*, without entering more deeply into any *Satz* after it has once been presented. Thus one thing relieves the other; we spend some time with everything, and then depart, having been stimulated by the variety. Whether we are elevated to a new and enduring perception of things [*Anschauung*] remains questionable. In the higher rondo forms it is especially the second subsidiary *Satz* that appears foreign amidst the rest of the content (no matter how happy an invention it may be and how suited to the rest), whereas the first and third groups [*Partie*], as shown in the last diagram, grow together into more solid unities, and the first subsidiary *Satz* in particular shows itself from two different perspectives (in two different keys).

If this lighter sense gives satisfaction, or if these misgivings are overcome by the power of the content, then the rondo form meets a purpose and conforms to reason. If not, then we must move beyond it.

The sonatina form

The first thing we can do is rid ourselves of the second subsidiary *Satz* – one would thus keep the first and third sections from the last diagram, without the middle section. We have become poorer and lighter but more unified.

This is the *sonatina form*. Its manner of origin (through subtraction) already indicates lightness and ephemerality; and in fact this is its particular character, one which has shown it to be suitable for many succinct and rapidly conceived overtures and the like.

The influence that this character may otherwise exercise, namely on modulation, must for now be left undiscussed. Let it merely be remarked that in this form, as in those that follow, instead of one main *Satz* sometimes two or three main *Sätze* and just as many subsidiary *Sätze* may appear, such that one must designate each of these *Satz*-successions (which, for the most part, stand together in the concord of the same key center) as main group [*Hauptpartie*] and subsidiary group [*Seitenpartie*]. {43}

The sonata form

The sonata form is more abundant; of all the stable configurations within the circle of homophonic forms, it is the richest.

It retains Parts I and III of the fifth rondo form but does not abandon the second part; thus it returns from the binary nature of the sonatina form back to a ternary nature. Yet the sonata form constructs its second part out of events from the first part, from the main *Satz*, the subsidiary *Satz*, or the closing *Satz*, or from two of the above, or from all of them.

Above all, it gains from this a higher unity.

Moreover, the *Sätze* that are repeated in the second part appear in a different order and in other keys; they are expanded, contracted, applied differently, manifoldly configured and deployed (this is why one refers technically to the second part as the "working through" [*Durcharbeitung*]), with the result that they arouse a more varied, more lasting, and deeper sympathy.

So much for the forms in which musical content appears uninterruptedly as "*one Satz*" (again taking this word in its expanded sense). My compositional method provides more information.

Let us now turn to polyphonic forms.

Polyphony

Any piece of music that consists of two or more voices, each (or several) of which having its own self-sufficient content and none of which being there merely as an accompaniment for the sake of a primary voice, is called polyphonic. It is as if each such voice presented an autonomous person – and the whole a drama.

There exists the possibility that the autonomy of the voices can go so far that none has anything in common with the others; but how could there then be an inner unity of the whole? The spirit of the artist that is united in itself will much rather mark the voices sounding together in a unitary work with a common idea or impulse – or by means of a firmly maintained opposition, as complementary beings (as persons or quasi-persons). Three main forms are distinguishable in accordance with the manner of content common to all the voices. This common content must be for one voice, so that each voice may reproduce it for itself.

Figuration

If the only thing shared by the polyphonic voices is the *impulse* of their motion – namely, a motive! (called a *figural motive*) – or even just the *approximate manner* of motion (of the melodic progression), then the form of *figuration* arises. Externally, such figuration may assume *Satz*-form, or two- or three-part song form, or it may be attached to a melody that is firmly self-sufficient and exists for itself. If the melody is a chorale tune, then the whole is called *chorale figuration*.

If two or more figural voices fall together in such a way that one borrows from the other more extended melodic groups (and not just a

motive of few tones), then the piece is called imitation.[14] {44}—Here
the imprecision of the distinction [between figuration and imitation]
resides in the imprecise nature of the forms.

The fugue

Incomparably more stable and more richly fashioned, the second polyphonic form makes its appearance: the *fugue*. Here the idea common to
all voices is not a mere motive, not an undetermined succession of tones
(a *Gang*), but rather a *Satz* that is closed and satisfying in and of itself; for
this reason it is preferably called a *theme* [*Thema*], or fugue theme.

The theme is given by one voice, repeated by a second (this is called
the answer), and wanders in this way through all the voices; each time
the theme travels through all (or several) of the voices it is called an
exposition [*Durchführung*].[15] Since it would prove tiresome to present
the theme constantly on the same scale degrees, one usually alternates,
and indeed primarily in such a way that the theme first appears in the
main key and then in that of the dominant. In the former it is called the
leader (*dux*), in the latter, the *companion* (*comes*). Although this is the first
best manner of alternation, it is by no means the only admissible manner
of presentation.

Any voice that has already been led in (or several of these voices)
continues on, sounding its own tune against the theme; this is called the
countersubject [*Gegensatz*]. At times it is necessary to spin the web of
voices some ways further before the theme can return; this is then called
an *episode*.

The essential task of the fugue is accomplished with the exposition;
one usually enlarges upon this, however, through the use of several ex-
positions, separated by episodes and changes of key.

Fugues in which two or three themes (which are then called subjects)
appear now at the same time and now in relief of each other are called
double and **triple fugues**. More on this belongs in my compositional
method.

The fugue unites a persistent lingering on the fundamental idea
(theme) with a greater variety in the working out – far greater, richer,

---

[14] Marx designates this category with both the German term *Nachahmung* and the Latinate term
Imitation.

[15] The word exposition is from our own tradition of fugue terminology. A more literal rendition
would be "leading-through."

and more significant throughout than has been indicated here. By virtue of meeting these two conditions, the fugue is the pinnacle of polyphonic art.[16]

The canon

Stricter, even less free than the fugue, is the canon, in which each successive voice takes up the tune of the previous voice completely, step for step, while the previous voice continues the tune further. Here we see the plan of a three-voice *canon*; the letters a b c d represent the content of the melody, divided into four (more or less) groups of the same duration:

1 a–b–c–d ....(d) x x x

2 ... a–b–c–d ....(d) x x

3 ....a–b–c–d ....(d) x

The second voice appears in the second temporal position with the first melodic group, sounding against the latter's second melodic group, {45} and so forth. If one finds it unsuitable to let the voices exit gradually – thus expressing the weakening of the whole – one may add a freely conceived appendix. It is indicated at the end of the above diagram by the letter x.

More on this and on the less important polyphonic forms must be omitted here. Thus our next category as well can be but briefly mentioned.

Union of homophony and polyphony

This comes about in two ways: either some merely accompanying voices may be added to a movement of polyphonic voices, or larger forms, namely the sonata form, may consist partly of homophonic and partly of polyphonic components. In the latter case, the use of polyphony is validated as an expression of more manifold and deeper content, content which does not find full satisfaction in the lonely lyricism

[16] Of course, these same two conditions – persistence of a fundamental idea and great variety in its treatment – characterize sonata form as well as it is presented in Marx's *Formenlehre*. Below, in the excerpt on sonata form from his compositional method, Marx will explicitly link these qualities with the alleged supremacy of sonata form. See pp. 93–98.

of homophony but rather adapts itself to the dramatic opposition and combination of various voices. Hardly any great work of any master dispenses with this higher power.

Each of the forms considered above offers its content in uninterrupted coherence; of course the song form with trio may count as an exception. As mentioned above, such an uninterruptedly coherent whole is called a *Satz* (used again in that more expansive sense).

Two or more such *Sätze* can now be linked to each other, more firmly or less firmly united, to form a greater structure.

The following forms are most worth mentioning here.

The variation

[This form consists of] a succession of repetitions of a *Liedsatz* (*theme*) in constantly altered presentations – the consideration of the same idea from different perspectives, its application in a different sense. More important is:

The sonata

[This consists of] the union of two, three, or more different movements into a greater whole.

Normally, three or four such movements succeed each other. The use of three movements has had an external but easily understood cause in the intention to alternate movements of lively and quiet character, faster and slower tempo, in order to have a more varied effect and to set both character types into relief. Thus a lively first movement (Allegro) is followed by a more peaceful one (Andante, Adagio), and the whole is closed with a *finale*, again in a more lively tempo. The richest of the homophonic (or mixed homophonic/polyphonic) forms, the sonata form, is usually chosen for the first movement. The andante (called the middle movement) takes song form or variation form, or one of the first rondo forms, or even sonata form (very narrowly {46} worked out), or it is fashioned figurally or fugally. The finale again takes up sonata form, one of the larger rondo forms, variation, or fugal form.

As a *fourth movement*, a lively movement in song form (*minuet* and trio) or a simpler rondo form (*scherzo*) is often added before or after the adagio. This is primarily done – e.g. in Haydn and Mozart – only for the sake of greater variety.

Intelligent art enthusiasts have broached the question: is either design, three-movement or four-movement, necessary – and why?

The number of movements is by no means a matter of necessity; not only would there be no reason to adduce for such a thing, but the experience of artists also speaks against this presumed necessity. First of all, two movements have often sufficed, if no motivation existed for a middle movement or for an opening allegro movement. Next, the number of movements has been exceeded, at least in a certain sense, through a more or less extensive *introductory movement* (introduction) – which, by the way, can also happen to any other compositional form. Finally, the number of essential movements has at times been exceeded (namely by Beethoven), as soon as some motivation existed to do so.

But even if necessity was lacking, should there not have been a deeper and determining impulse for those predominant configurations, by far the majority, whether or not one was ever conscious of the same?—

This impulse appears to be succinctly contained in the following. The artist approaches his new construction [*Bildung*] with freshly gathered power, kindled and elevated by a newly awakened creative urge. This he pours forth in his first movement, which is thus brought to an animated and richly wrought completion. —Yet through this access of creativity and its elevating power, the artist's own interior has been as if newly revealed; he looks into himself, submerges himself in this new world that he has found within himself: this is the thoughtful, quiet adagio. And only now does he return, freshly rejuvenated, to life and productive activity in the finale, cheerfully at peace or with renewed power for struggle and victory, or with whatever the newly experienced day may bring.[17]

If the artist has experienced a deeper transformation within himself and then turns his gaze from his interior submersion back out into the world, then even the world itself will seem foreign and alienating to him. He knew it before and recognizes it again – and it appears as an Other to him, for he has become other. This schism, softened by the feeling of his own elevation and ascendancy over that which has become alien, finds its expression in the humor of the scherzo.

This is a psychological evolution obvious in a great many works (per-

---

[17] Note again how Marx associates the left-to-right process of music with the creative intentions and/or psychological process of the artist.

haps the majority).[18] But one need only consider Beethoven's "Les adieux" sonata or his "Pastoral" Symphony to realize that motivation of a completely different sort can take its place.

On the whole, we have up to now found more or less determined forms for {47} a similar course of ideas or feelings. But subjective self-determination, indeed even caprice (as mentioned above), have their own right as well.

SINGULAR FORMS [*EINZELFORMEN*]

The right of subjective self-determination makes its appearance in these forms, which we designate with the name *singular* because every single work that belongs in this category is fashioned in complete autonomy according to the impulse of its creator, without needing to connect to or approach any other work.

The fantasia

The fantasia is the prototype of all such works. It consists of a thoroughly free linking of *Sätze* in any number, form, or size, according to one's wishes.

In this category belong all those metamorphoses of established forms that have their origin in completely isolated and subjectively manifested impulses or intentions of the artist. Yet even in these apparently arbitrary constructions (so long as they are not aberrations) artistic reason thoroughly prevails. My composition treatise and my "Music in the nineteenth century" (theory of method [*Methodik*]) provide reams of examples of this.

Let us cast a last glance upon the *material* in which the artist's idea is embodied, if only to mark the most salient points.

Instrumental music makes do throughout with the forms we have considered and with those we have overlooked on account of their lack of importance. The quartet, the quintet, etc., and the symphony all take the form of a sonata, but are worked out at times more refinedly, at times

---

[18] For more on Marx's view of the psychological scenario inherent in the three- or four-movement sonata, see *Die Lehre von der musikalischen Komposition*, 5th edn (Leipzig: Breitkopf und Härtel, 1879), vol. 3, 319–33, and Ian Bent, ed. *Music Analysis in the Nineteenth Century*, vol. 2: *Hermeneutic Approaches* (Cambridge: Cambridge University Press, 1994), 215.

more grandly and more powerfully, and even more polyphonically, always in accordance with the capability and significance of the instrumental means.

In the *motet* and in the *opera finale*, vocal music enjoys the same freedom of formal arrangement we found above in the fantasia; for the rest, it uses all the established forms, from song to sonata form, while it nevertheless finds means, in the guiding power of the word, of reaching its goal more rapidly than instrumental music, thus simplifying and abbreviating the forms. In this respect, the historical evolution of the *aria form* is particularly enlightening as to the essence of form; perhaps nowhere else is the correspondence between form and the spiritual direction of the artist more distinctly discernible. At the creation of opera (the beginning of the seventeenth century), the aria appeared in a more compact song form, succinctly tailored to the rhetorical (Giulio Caccini) or the pathetic (Jacopo Peri) expression of the word, for this was the necessary task of the age. As opera very soon thereafter turned to more lavish pleasures, the urge to indulge oneself in tones predominated. Plastically expansive forms, coloratura, and variety in performances now familiar and commodious were all desired and attained; the aria settled, sonata-like, into broadly separate sections: an expansively detailed allegro, adagio, and return of the allegro. The most recent Italians continue to generate this form in their arias and duets. As Gluck turned to the truth {48} of dramatic and verbal expression, and as Mozart began to master a musical expression that was deeper and more rapidly affecting, the aria form contracted into a tighter, more solid kernel; the majority of their successors became more dissolute formally, because musical content did not care to concentrate itself more energetically in their spirits.

Recitative

If song dissolves words and music together, in the recitative musical life enters into the word and is subordinate to the power of speech.

Melodrama

In the melodrama, musical life lingers as a foreign, enveloping element for the still untransformed word, such that here too mediating forms [*Zwischenformen*] lead from the word as used in free speech to the word that has merged with music.

And, to touch on one last thing, though music has long been called, and rightly so, the art of the soul and its motion, yet, in the social forms of the *dance* and the *march* and in that mirrored image of real life, the *drama*, music enters into a fully warranted alliance with outside life, just as our inner natures cannot escape the influence of outside life and their own retrospective influence upon that life.

REVIEW

The forms of music were not to be presented here exhaustively; it goes without saying that even the forms that have existed up to now may be transformed and increased. Yet the above must already serve to justify the idea from which we have proceeded, concerning the rationality and thus necessity of these forms. This rationality is revealed not merely as demonstrated above, in single forms, or in every single form, but also – and still more pronouncedly – in the persevering work of the spirit: ready, as if for every possible task, and in all directions, to impress its content into stable forms, and to do so always in accordance with that content.

One can be in need of this or that form; one can dispense with this or that form – namely, if the content that conditions it is lacking. To renounce a form arbitrarily: this is to limit or falsify one's spirit in that direction. To renounce form *per se*: this is to return to spiritual chaos. To avoid cultivation and instruction in musical forms, hoping to replace these with one's own power: this is to bear the work of millennia and of all the masters upon one's own shoulders, to create the world all over again. "*[The world] has already been created!*" It is simply a matter of making oneself at home there, of living there.

Prof. Dr. A. B. Marx

A PRACTICAL AND THEORETICAL METHOD OF MUSICAL COMPOSITION, VOL. III: SELECTED EXCERPTS

Once Marx reaches sonata form in the progression of forms he unfolds in the compositional method, he lingers there for some hundred pages, treating sonata form first in broad strokes and then in greater detail. His nearly exclusive use of Beethoven's piano sonatas as models for his discussion illustrates his belief that sonata form found its highest realization in the hands of Beethoven. Hence the lavish detail, for in this survey of what he felt were some of the greatest existing realizations of the greatest possible musical form Marx has reached the pinnacle of his *Formenlehre*, and he will not soon abandon it.

Immediately preceding the excerpted discussion, Marx surveys the rondo forms, presenting them as an evolving series of forms that is then crowned by sonata form. As we observed in "Form in music," Marx considers the distinguishing feature of this family of forms to be the motion-oriented alternation of thematic utterance (*Satz*) and transitional passage (*Gang*). The rondo forms can be represented schematically as follows (MS = main *Satz* [*Hauptsatz*]; SS = subsidiary *Satz* [*Seitensatz*]; CS = closing *Satz* [*Schlusssatz*]; G = *Gang*):

First Rondo Form	MS G MS
Second Rondo Form	MS SS (G) MS
Third Rondo Form	MS SS1 G MS SS2 G MS
Fourth Rondo Form	MS SS1 G MS SS2 G MS SS1
Fifth Rondo Form	MS SS1 G CS SS2 G MS SS1 G CS

Marx refers to the three large sections of sonata form not as exposition, development, and recapitulation but simply as First Part, Second Part, and Third Part. These designations help him show the relation of sonata form to the foregoing fourth and fifth rondo forms, where he also distinguishes three large parts. Another, perhaps more important, aspect of his rationale for not using terms like development and recapitulation can be gleaned from his footnote on p. 94.

For the sake of space, the self-composed examples that Marx uses to illustrate each main point in the first part of his discussion have been omitted, along with any commentary specifically applying to them. Compensating this regrettable omission is the fact that all of the many examples featuring passages from Beethoven's piano sonatas have been retained in the second part of Marx's discussion.

Die Lehre von der musikalischen Komposition, praktisch-theoretisch, 4th edn (Leipzig: Breitkopf und Härtel, 1868), Vol. III (Applied Composition), Book Six (Instrumental Composition), Part Four

SONATA FORM

{201} The loose concatenation of various *Sätze* and *Gänge* appeared as a character trait of the rondo forms. In the rondo, at first only one *Satz*, the main *Satz*, was important enough to be repeated; it thus stood as the only fixed part of the whole, and for precisely that reason always had to be brought back in essentially the same manner and in the same key. Thus it provided an element of constancy; but at the same time, the frequent returns to the same point kept the modulations from developing more freely and energetically, limiting them almost exclusively to the spaces between main and subsidiary *Sätze*.

The fourth, and especially the fifth, rondo forms went beyond this confining cycle. Because they join main and subsidiary *Sätze* into a more unified whole, especially in the Third Part, where they bring them back (with the closing *Satz*, if there is one) closely bound together by the main key, one recognizes in these forms another, and higher, orientation. That which is *separate* (individual *Sätze*) is no longer valid in *isolation*; rather, the intimate union of separate parts (individual *Sätze*) in a whole – the *whole* in its inner *unity* – becomes the main concern. In such a whole the isolated [*Satz*] begins to lose its rigidity; it is no longer there merely for itself, nor must it hold to its place, staying within itself: it now moves (at least the first subsidiary *Satz* moves) from its original spot to another position (from the dominant or relative key to the main key), and it does so for the sake of the whole, which now wants to close with greater unity and with more material in the main key.

Only the second subsidiary *Satz* has stayed aloof from this tendency. It exists for itself, as a foreign element between the First and Third Parts. If one were to remove the second subsidiary *Satz* and its appendages (*Gang* and pedal point) [from the fourth or fifth rondo form], the First and Third Parts together would form a musical work of a much more confirmed {202} unity than is offered by any of the rondo forms ...

The *sonata form*[1] completes what the fourth and fifth rondo forms have begun. Generally speaking, it does this in a twofold manner. First, it gives up (for purely formal reasons, as suggested above) the foreign element (the second subsidiary *Satz*) that the fifth rondo form still maintains between the now amalgamated First and Third Parts, and restricts itself to these more closely unified sections [*Partien*]. This results in the *small sonata form*, or *sonatina form*. Next, it forms a new Second, or middle, Part — one unified with the First Part and indeed made from the same content. This results in *sonata form proper*.

Both forms, or better, both manners of the one sonata form are used for fast as well as slow movements. We will study sonata form first in fast movements, since it is here, where motion from one section to the other predominates along with the liveliness of the sections themselves, that the nature of the form is most clearly revealed ...

Two sections on sonatina form follow the above introductory discussion: Section One — Sonatina form; Section Two — Closer details of sonatina form.

SECTION THREE: SONATA FORM

{220} It immediately becomes apparent that sonatina form is one of those transitional configurations that are indeed justified and necessary both internally and in the sequence of all art forms, but in which a distinct formal concept has not yet reached full ripeness.

The sonatina strove beyond the rondo forms to a more intimate unity of content; but it achieved this by {221} sacrificing a section of the content of those earlier forms — the second subsidiary *Satz* — with a

---

[1] [Marx:] As is well known, *sonata* means ... a musical work for one (or two) instruments, made by joining several separate movements together, e.g. allegro, adagio, scherzo, and finale. Lacking another name already in currency, however, we designate with the name *sonata form* the wholly determinate form of a single movement. The name "allegro" or "allegro form," which is used now and again, is already rendered unsuitable by the fact that the sonata form is frequently used for slow movements as well.

consequent lessening of significance. And, then again, it was inclined to insert a transitional or bridge passage in place of the omitted part; this proves that the rejected second part had its own justification. But that which is inserted in its place cannot truly replace it. Thus this form is good only for cursory constructions.

This observation leads directly to sonata form itself and its essential character trait: sonata form cannot dispense with a *middle section* (between the first and last of the sonatina); it must assume a *three-part* form. But this middle, or second, part may not introduce *foreign* material – a second subsidiary *Satz* – as in the rondo forms, for this would disrupt the unity whose complete attainment is in fact the task of the sonata. Consequently, the Second Part[2] of sonata form must hold to the content of the First Part, either *exclusively*, or at least *primarily*.

Thus the main features of the new form are arranged as follows:

Part 1	Part 2	Part 3
MS SS G CS	— — —	MS SS G CS

One recognizes immediately that the first and last parts, broadly speaking, are familiar from the fifth rondo form and the sonatina form; only the middle part is essentially new.

Before progressing to this part, which is the most important object of this stage of our study, we will undertake several considerations already resulting from a {222} preliminary view of the form.

First. Let us imagine a piece of music that holds to its main and subsidiary *Sätze* through *three* parts: we must acknowledge a deeper meaning in such persistent content than was the case with sonatina form. Or, in other words, the composer must be more compelled by these *Sätze*, he must feel predisposed to work with them more intently.

---

[2] [Marx:] According to the usual terminology, only two parts are recognized in those pieces written in sonata form. The First Part, which is usually repeated and discernibly isolated by the repeat sign, is treated as such; everything else, i.e. the Second and Third Parts together, are treated as a single Second Part – this is often the case with the fifth rondo form. But the separation of the Second and Third Parts is, as we already know, so essential that we cannot neglect it without distorting our considered view of the form and losing sight of its basis in reason. This has been felt earlier as well, for within the so-called Second Part (the joined Second and Third Parts) the return of the main theme and everything further has been called the *reprise*, while that which precedes the reprise was called the *working-through*. This would indeed mean three parts with an essential separation of the third from the second! Yet the names seem less than exact (the Third Part is in no way a mere reprise or repetition, and working-through takes place in all parts and moreover in many other art forms), and this practice lumps together in the Second Part things which must only be separated again at once, creating an incidental hindrance to study.

Thus *Sätze* that are indeed suited only for that slighter form appear too inconsequential for the higher sonata form ...

Second. The mere act of repeating a *Satz* already shows an inclination to hold fast to it, as if it were a possession. Thus in the rondo forms the main theme especially served as a stationary touchpoint of the whole, to which one returned in order to repeat it again and again. A higher interest is manifest in the sonata form. No longer satisfied to bring back such a *Satz* as if it were a dead possession, it enlivens it instead, lets it undergo variation and be repeated in different manners and with different destinations: it transforms the *Satz* into *an Other*, which is nonetheless recognized as the offspring of the first *Satz* and which stands in for it ... The rondo cannot entertain essential alterations of its *Sätze*, but only peripheral changes, whereas the sonata form can embrace these as well ...

In these transformations, obviously, lies the power to stimulate a more varied and intensified interest in the *Satz* ... For this reason it is possible to elevate a *Satz* that is in itself less significant to the status of a worthy and satisfying subject for the larger form. Indeed, the power of the form and of the composer not infrequently shows itself {223} to great advantage precisely with those beginnings that appear less important at first blush – although it seems *inartistic* to search out such a *Satz* deliberately, in order to put one's artistic talent on its mettle, and *negligent* to take up the first best idea and go to work without feeling called to it or excited by it. One of the happiest examples of this sort is offered by the first movement of Beethoven's G major Sonata, Op. 31. The main theme, spilling over with genial humor, has this as its germ:

Example 4.1

Were this to stand for itself, alone and unvaried, one could certainly deem it full of energy but not of significance. Yet under its stimulus the spirit of the artist rings upon it the most ingenious changes, in wonderful succession; they take hold of us ever more profoundly, finally offering even milder intimations to our unexpectedly moved souls. —To assume that the master chose his *Satz* for such a play of technical facility would be to award him paltry praise befitting a schoolboy. There was no question of technique here: for the artist there is no technique. That which the artistic spirit seizes becomes its own – under the sway of fervent love it becomes a precious and vital witness to that spirit. This can be seen and proved with this *Beethovenian Satz*, as it can with every art work, and every artist knows it. Technique – outward skill or, worse, vainglorious play – has nothing to do with such artistic love.

Third. That light and capricious, even superficial, manner in which the sonatina form springs from the half cadence of its main *Satz* into the subsidiary *Satz* and its key center can no longer suffice in the higher sonata form, where the whole is thoroughly permeated and conditioned by the urge for a unified, powerful sense of forward and progressive motion. {224} A formal transition is now necessary, one that will lead us unequivocally from the realm of the main *Satz* into that of the subsidiary *Satz* and then confirm the latter.

To this end, and in accordance with long recognized precepts, there is a modulation *in the First Part* from the main theme and its key to the dominant of the dominant, and from there back to the dominant ... {225} In movements in minor, as we also know by now, the modulation would ordinarily go not to the dominant but to the relative major ...

From these easily settled points we now turn to the most important point, to the construction of the Second Part, which demands separate consideration.

SECTION FOUR: THE SECOND PART OF SONATA FORM

As has already been established, the Second Part of a sonata form contains in essence no new content.

As a consequence it must concern itself principally with the content of the First Part – that is, with the main *Satz*, with the subsidiary *Satz*, and even with the closing *Satz* – and indeed it may deal with only one *Satz*, with two, or even with all of them.

{226} Yet this involvement is in no way simply a matter of repetition, as in the handling of the main *Satz* in the rondo. The reappearing themes are rather *chosen, ordered and connected*, and *varied*, in ways suitable to each different stage of the composition.

Thus it is clear that the Second Part manifests itself primarily as the locus of variety and motion, and once again we see the original antithesis, the fundamental law of all musical formation now revealed in the three parts of the sonata form: rest—motion—rest.

The motivation for greater variety in the ordering and disposition of the material lies in the character of the Second (or motion-oriented) Part. Its general task is as follows: to lead, with material selected from the First Part, from the conclusion of the First Part to the pedal point on the dominant of the main key, and then to the entrance of the Third Part.

Variety is chiefly found, however, in the linkage [*Anknüpfung*], the way one leads from the First Part, then in the carrying-through[3] [*Durchführung*] of content that is wholly or at least primarily borrowed from the First Part.

It would hardly be possible and certainly unnecessary to enumerate, much less to begin sketching out, all the typical and unusual procedures that may be used in the Second Part of sonata form; we can only be permitted to limit ourselves to the most important, those which suggest the main tendencies ...

> Here and in the next two sections, Marx discusses, with many home-made musical examples, different ways of beginning the Second Part: with an immediate return to the main *Satz* (Section Four), with an entirely new *Satz* (Section Five), with a closing *Satz* that refers back to the main *Satz*, with an independent closing *Satz*, or with a "*Gang*-like" introduction (Section Six).
>
> In Section Four, Marx considers the choice of tonalities suitable for use when starting the Second Part with the main *Satz*, deciding that since one cannot use the dominant or the tonic, tonic minor would work, as would the relative minor of the dominant.

{228} If we look back for a moment to the rondo forms, we see that the sonata form's distinguishing difference as well as the process of its unfolding – as energetic as it is more unified – are put in the most unequivocal light with the first gesture of the Second Part. Here too the main *Satz* appears for a second time, as in the third and fourth rondo forms, and will again appear, perhaps unaltered, in the Third Part. But it has become something else, and not just in peripheral aspects of the accompaniment but indeed in its essential features (even in mode). We

---

[3] This term tries to capture both the sense of leading-through and the sense of carrying out, or executing; both senses are implied in the word *Durchführung* – before it simply became the equivalent of our musico-formal designation "development."

may indeed deem these changes essential, for, as has been shown, they are called for by the very conditions under which the main *Satz* is constrained to reappear. That the main *Satz* must avoid its initial key here as assiduously as it had to maintain it in the rondo forms was already decisive; the principle {229} of motion, of progress, was thereby elevated over the subordinate principle of stability manifest in the rondo forms …

SECTION SEVEN: SUPPLEMENTARY REMARKS ON THE WORKING OUT OF THE SECOND PART

{244} Since the manner of introducing the Second Part forms an integral whole with the way the rest of it is realized, we have treated its further continuation simultaneously with the various ways of beginning it, in accordance with the practical tendency and method of this entire book.

But we had to direct our attention primarily to the introduction, covering the rest in the shortest and simplest way, in order to attain an overview of the Second Part, and to do so repeatedly, even if the full range of its configurations could not be demonstrated.[4]

{245} Under these circumstances several supplementary hints on the working out of the Second Part are now called for, which will require but few words.

1 To begin with, it goes without saying that all the important features we have demonstrated in the Second Part can appear in greater fullness and expanse than in this textbook, where for the sake of space the tersest exposition – only enough to shed some light – must have priority over a richer and more extensive treatment. In particular, the transitions and pedal points will usually need further realization. It is hoped that our examples will suffice, since by now it should be clear that nothing is easier than the continuation of a transitional passage or a pedal point once it has been initiated; how much farther one ought to go must be decided in accordance with the particular ten-

---

[4] In the several examples of Second-Part procedures that Marx presents in Sections Four through Six, he often brings his Second Part in rather short order to the dominant pedal point that will usher in the Third Part. He thus discusses in depth only the various manners of beginning the Second Part, giving the rest short shrift. The examples from Beethoven introduced in the next section provide a more complete picture of his conception of the Second Part, however.

dency of each case. The only general advice we can give is: that one would do well – if particular considerations of content and mood do not demand otherwise – to grant a certain symmetrical proportion or equipoise to the various sections, such that the Second Part is *approximately* as long as the First, the returning main or subsidiary theme groups *approximately* match the preceding or subsequent transitional material, and so forth. This balanced formation expresses the even-handed sympathy and overview that the composer should extend to all the sections of his creation, and it calls forth the pleasant feeling of a just and secure sovereignty in the listener as well, even if the latter is not equipped to keep tally of such things and is perhaps not even at all aware of the whole organism that so pleases and benefits him.— Yet the urge to achieve such proportion must never degenerate into an anxious *tallying* and *counting* of measures, above all during composition; this would be the death of any artistic impulses. Even back in [our discussion of] song form, a much more limited and easily surveyable territory, we moved beyond exact proportion to a general sense of proportion, and became convinced that the former was not necessary for the pleasant and rational effect of the latter. If we allowed ourselves even there to answer four bars with five or six, and so forth, then a few bars more or less matters still less here, in compositions so much larger and more complex.

2 We know already from our treatment of polyphony {246} that transitions and themes can be formed or continued polyphonically as well as homophonically. Thus it is obvious that in the sonata form as well, and particularly in the carrying-through of pre-existing *Sätze* and transitional motives that forms the Second Part, one can make extensive use of polyphony. As is well known, polyphony enables us to give a whole new meaning to a theme, especially by means of the types of inversion … , to gain an entirely new perspective on a familar theme, and to lend the whole, even in the midst of all these configural changes, a unity and solidity hardly possible in larger realizations except through the use of polyphonic techniques …

3 Thus it follows that one can even make use of the fugue in carrying out the Second Part. It is clear, however, that no actual, self-sufficient fugue can occur here but merely the use of fugal technique for some particular part of the section.

Neither the main nor the subsidiary *Satz* can serve as the subject of the fugue; it must be formed from motives taken from these *Sätze*, chiefly from their beginnings. In most cases the choice would have to fall on the main *Satz*, since, for reasons already known, it tends to have the most energetic and thus most promising configuration for the fugue.[5] Yet we can form no rule from this; very often the subsidiary *Satz* is better suited for the formation of a fugue subject, or better fits the mood of the composition as the Second Part progresses ...

{247} 4 Finally one must mention that at times the Second Part not only begins with the continuation of the closing *Satz* but is exclusively dedicated to the carrying-through of this *Satz*. This occurs whenever the closing *Satz* is the most compelling to the composer, and the main and subsidiary *Sätze* are less in need of any further working through because of their constitution – if, for example, they contain an oft-repeated germinal {248} *Satz* and were thus displayed with sufficient variety already at their first appearance ... Anyone who understands in general how to develop a *Satz* ... will remain indifferent as to whether the *Satz* to be developed was originally a closing *Satz* or some other.

In any event, one must regard this case as exceptional, since it places the center of gravity on a secondary *Satz* instead of on one of the primary sections (main *Satz* or subsidiary *Satz*).

SECTION EIGHT: THE THIRD PART OF SONATA FORM

Concerning the formation of the Third Part of sonata form there is little to add to what was said in the section on the fifth rondo form ... since the Third Part is essentially shaped just like the Third Part of that rondo form.

It begins with the main *Satz* repeated in its entirety, even altered at some especially suitable point, and perhaps – especially if the Second Part dealt more with the subsidiary or closing *Sätze* – further realized ...

{249} The subsidiary *Satz* follows the main *Satz* ... and indeed in the main key; touching on the keys of the subdominant and dominant serves, as we know, to make the main key's establishment here all the more decisive ... The allusion to the first of these keys can be easily

[5] The reasons that Marx considers the main *Satz* to be more energetic than the subsidiary *Satz* will be made clear in the succeeding section, "A closer discussion of sonata form."

dispatched, or even completely omitted, if this key was heavily stressed in the Second Part.

This modulation [through the subdominant and dominant back to the main key] is fashioned differently according to the particular circumstances of each individual piece.

In most cases it takes place within the main theme, by leading it onward as a transition ...

At times, when the main *Satz* is firmly closed, a special transitional passage or a chain of *Sätze* [*Satzkette*] will be appended, and the modulation to the subdominant is achieved just as the modulation to the dominant of the dominant was in the First Part.

Sometimes it may seem appropriate to introduce the subsidiary *Satz* simply at first, but then to modulate with it to the subdominant and from there through the dominant back again to the main key ...

{250} At other times, this spot can be used − like a kind of supplement to the Second Part − for another working out of the main *Satz* or its motives, if the main *Satz* seems especially momentous or fertile, or if it has not been treated in the Second Part ...

{251} Finally, the closing *Satz* too, or the *Gang* that precedes it, can be expanded or an extension may be added that brings the main *Satz* to the fore once again. All such expansions do not belong to the essence of the form and are not necessary, so they can easily become a nuisance. One must indeed weigh every single case to determine whether there is a call for such enlargements, whether the *Sätze* need and are worthy of repeated entrances and realizations − and whether such reiterations in the Third Part are sufficiently important to justify their presence.

Die Lehre von der musikalischen Komposition, praktisch-theoretisch, 2nd edn (Leipzig: Breitkopf und Härtel, 1848), Vol. III (Applied Composition), Book Six, Part Five

A CLOSER DISCUSSION OF SONATA FORM

{247} In the previous part our task was to lead the student as directly as possible to the possession of a form whose importance will become ever more apparent as we press on. But this quick pace made it impossible to attain a fully sufficient knowledge; and had we been inclined toward exhaustive examination rather than toward leading the student back to creative work as quickly as possible, it would have been contrary to the fundamental principle of a true method of art [*Kunstlehre*] (which in this respect is essentially distinct from a pure or, preferably, a *scientific method*). For this reason, we held almost exclusively to a single model, seen from various perspectives.[1]

From this point on, we are obliged to engage in a closer discussion, a demonstration through works of the masters. By experiencing the works of others after actually practicing the above fundamental precepts, discernment and practical ability will ripen together, evenly and insepa-rably. The former will not be allowed to turn into abstract knowledge, both dead and deadly for the artist; the latter will avoid a merely empiri-cal mimicry (constantly threatened by onesidedness and mannerism).

SECTION ONE: THE MAIN *SATZ*

Regarding the content of the main *Satz*, we will determine not only its general form, but also the particular manner of its execution and then its further progress up to the entrance of the subsidiary *Satz*, as well as the manner of the latter. The main *Satz* had a similar significance already in the rondo forms; we can now build further on that knowledge.

We found that the main *Sätze* of the initial rondo forms most often assumed two- or three-part song form; yet already in the fourth, and still more in the fifth rondo form, we had cause to prefer a more mobile formation.

This is also the case with sonata form. This form can present the main *Satz* just as frequently – and, when it will, even more frequently – than any rondo form. But it displaces the main *Satz*, transforms it, blends it with the remaining sections [*Partien*] of the piece into an inwardly uni-fied {248} whole; *it will not let the main Satz stand still*, as happens in the rondo, but rather *moves it*, to other keys, to other *Sätze* and *Gänge*. For this the two- and three-part song form is much too firmly closed and steady; one will never, or only in unusual cases (the author cannot think of any), find it applied, or applicable, to sonata form.

---

[1] This single model was Marx's "workshop" example of a sonata-form movement for piano.

The *Satz*-form

The sonata much prefers to grant the *Satz*-form to its main idea. Yet this most constricted of all the closed forms would have too little weight to sustain the main idea of a larger and richer piece of music. Thus it becomes necessary 1) to expand the *Satz* internally, and 2) to fortify the *Satz* through repetition.

This is Beethoven's procedure in his genial Sonata in E♭, Op. 29 or 31.[2]

Example 4.2[3]

This is the *Satz* that serves as main *Satz* and as the main idea of the whole piece. Though it seems narrowly limited for this task, we should not overlook the fact that it already possesses a content unusually rich for a *Satz*. The first bar is repeated; the next motive (contained in the two following bars) is repeated and led forth; the whole consists of eight bars and embraces at least three different motives, reckoning the seventh bar as one of them. — It follows that not every *Satz* is suitable for our purposes; instead of the *Satz* in its lowest stage, a more developed and thus enriched *Satz* is required ...

This *Satz* must now be imprinted in accordance with the increased importance of its purpose and the richness of its content; it must become more imposing. — Beethoven thus takes off from its final tone with this *Gang*:

Example 4.3

---

[2] Marx is referring, of course, to Op. 31, No. 3. (The sonata may have been known in some catalogs as Op. 29.)

[3] [Marx:] Here and in most of the following examples excerpts, however abbreviated and highlighted, can and must suffice.

{249} He then repeats his *Satz*, such that its first bar, as Example 4.3 implies, appears up high, its second bar (the repetition of the first) an octave lower, the two following bars one octave lower still, the next two bars two octaves higher, and the last bars in the old register (as in Example 4.2, an octave below the previous two bars). In this way, the whole, hovering above and below its original position, immediately assumes the mobility that characterizes sonata form...

But the composer is still not satisfied; he now takes his first motive and builds another *Satz* from it — something like an appendix to what came before:

Example 4.4

Then he repeats this too. Thus one *Satz* (reckoning Example 4.4 with Example 4.2) has already spread over twenty-five bars and has both imprinted its content and shown itself to be more mobile and progressive [*fortschreitender*] than was possible with the song form in several parts, or even the period. This mobility resides in the repeated closings and in the constant transformation of the same content; one stage after the other is dismissed, and the returning material newly shaped. And even after all this, we shall discover that the composer still has not let go of his *Satz*.

In other respects, however, our example as it stands is not entirely unequivocal. The formation in Example 4.4 is indeed thoroughly derived from the main motive of the actual *Satz* (in Example 4.2) and may thus be deemed a mere appendix; yet it can just as well be seen as a *Satz* in and of itself. If one wants to entertain this latter interpretation, then the case would not belong under the present rubric but would be covered in our last category.[4]

---

[4] This is the category of the *Satz*-chain. See below, p. 112.

Beethoven's *Pathétique Sonata*, Op. 13, offers a more sharply pronounced example – even if it, too, does not stand beyond all doubt. The main idea is a broadly laid out *Satz* that closes completely in the tonic.

Example 4.5

{250} At the arrival of the cadence, the same music repeats up to its eighth bar and then quickly turns to the dominant.

Example 4.6

This is a transition into the key of the dominant with a full cadence; but it is held so fleetingly that one can credit it only with the effect of a half cadence …

The advantages of the *Satz* for sonata form are already apparent, making it clear that *Satz*-form will be a more propitious and satisfying form for the main *Satz* than will the period, our next category.

The period

Let us observe one such period, which serves as the main *Satz* of *Dussek*'s E♭ major Sonata, Op. 75.

Example 4.7

We find that the idea is so securely and satisfactorily closed through the balanced formation of antecedent and consequent phrases and through their corresponding cadences (the last triad of the antecedent, marked with an asterisk, is broadened into a dominant chord [i.e. a dominant-seventh chord] through the logical progression of the melody), that there remains within it no impulse at all for further progress ... And it should be emphasized that this has nothing to do with the perhaps lesser degree of interest that its content arouses in us when compared with the Beethoven; it rather finds its sole cause in the closure-oriented form [of the period].

For this reason, the composer (to whom this idea must indeed have been worthy, or he would not have retained it) finds no opportunity to develop something from it, to lead it further, {251} or to repeat it, but rather adds an appendix, somewhat in the manner of a closing *Satz*:

Example 4.8

This finally begins to move but then leads no further.

Beethoven finds himself in the same situation in his C major Sonata, Op. 2, in which there is no lack of lively animation nor of more inward interest. The main *Satz* has a periodic form, although in a most concentrated brevity:

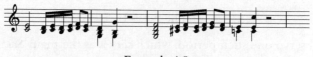

Example 4.9

For this reason, it too leads no further. Thus a new *Satz* is formed – and indeed from the same motive, as if it were an appendix.

Example 4.10

It is then repeated, with the melody transposed to the bass, and – once again – closed. This *Satz*, too, could lead no further, since its inherent interest has already been exhausted through itself and through the period from which it emerged as an appendix.

From this we may now understand an oft-taken turn. In and of itself, the *Satz* tends to be less than satisfactory, whereas the period tends to be too closed. As we have long recognized, this latter effect is indeed due to the closure of its consequent phrase, which is prepared and reinforced by that of the antecedent phrase. It thus becomes a matter of uniting the advantages of the *Satz* with those of the period; this is achieved by our next category.

The period with open [*aufgelöst*] consequent phrase

Namely, a regular antecedent phrase is formed and the consequent begun with motives from the same; but the latter is not brought to a periodic cadence but led beyond, in the manner of a *Gang*, to the subsidiary *Satz*. In such a case, however, the antecedent phrase, as the sole actual core of the main theme group, is represented with sufficient plenitude. Let us consider several examples of *Beethoven*.

We take our *first* from the small F minor Sonata, Op. 2. {252}

Example 4.11

We have before us a *Satz* from which the main group [*Hauptpartie*] will form, and indeed an *antecedent Satz*, since the cadence falls on the dominant.[5] The consequent phrase begins with the main motive (marked

---

[5] [Marx:] Of course the harmonic progression digresses somewhat: in the second half of the seventh bar the sixth chord b♭–d♭–g is inserted between the tonic and dominant triads; were the succession of sixth chords not so flowing, one would have expected b♭–d♭–f here (as a cadence leading from the subdominant to the dominant).

with a in Example 4.11) and then plays some more with the second
motive (b in Example 4.11):

Example 4.12

This finds no closure but runs, *Gang*-like, into the subsidiary *Satz*.

A second example is provided by the main *Satz* from the finale of the
C♯ minor Sonata, Op. 27. It begins as follows:

Example 4.13

In this fashion, the antecedent phrase of an otherwise regular period, that which serves as a
main *Satz* for Beethoven's lovely F major Sonata (Op. 10), is steered toward a cadence in the
subdominant through the irrepressible flow of the melody, whereas the periodic form clearly
appears in the rest (the first four bars are a prelude …; the four following bars form the
antecedent phrase of the period).

Example 4.11a

{253} Thus it ends with a half cadence (the figured bass numbering is not even exact here; only that which is most necessary is indicated) – or with a cadence in the dominant that has only the significance of a half cadence – and with this presents itself as an antecedent phrase. And in fact a consequent phrase also seems to want to form; it sets out again with the main motive (bars 1 and 2 in Example 4.13). Only instead of bringing itself and the entire period to a firm close, this consequent leads, *Gang*-like, to the subsidiary *Satz* in G♯ minor (the dominant minor for the relative major).[6]

These sorts of formations unite mobility, offered by a *Satz* that quickly breaks off and then is repeated or varied, with the inner coherence and closed nature of a period. The antecedent phrase of Example 4.11 taken with the consequent phrase of Example 4.12, or the antecedent phrase of Example 4.13 and its consequent, are more coherent than even the *Sätze* in Examples 4.2 and 4.4, although these latter proceed from one and the same motive. And these [period-like constructions] are also dispatched relatively quickly and *avoid* the uniformity of several cadences of the same sort: whereas Example 4.2 closes on E♭, as does its repetition, as well as the consequent phrase in Example 4.4, Example 4.11 closes on the dominant C while its consequent (Example 4.12) leads to A♭ and will then go even further, to E♭, before the subsidiary *Satz* arrives in A♭.

The enlarged period

The enlarged period offers similar advantages, even when it closes in a truly periodic fashion – and still more when its consequent phrase, like those above, opens out into a *Gang*.

The deeply felt first movement of Beethoven's E minor Sonata, Op. 90, offers an example of the first sort. Here is the period of the main *Satz*, sparsely abstracted: {254}

[6] Another very striking example of this type of structure, although leading to the relative major, would be the opening of the Fifth Symphony.

Example 4.14

The main motive spreads out over four subsections [*Abschnitte*] (a, b, c, d) of two bars each, going from E minor through D to G major, and from G major through F♯ to B minor. A fifth subsection (e, in two parts) lingers in G major; a sixth (f), derived from e, finally makes a half cadence in the tonic key. A consequent phrase (g) of four bars presents itself to this broad, sixteen-bar antecedent phrase (if such a designation is still valid) and, in order to suffice, must be repeated after a deceptive cadence.

With this, the idea is indeed closed off with as much satiation and as little need of further continuation as that Dussek period from Example 4.7. This can convince us that even in the case of the Dussek the hindrance to further continuation is not, say, its less interesting content but rather the choice of form. And yet Beethoven's many-limbed period has within it all the motion and variety that befits a sonata.

In the main *Satz* of Beethoven's great C major Sonata, Op. 53, we see an enlarged period with a flowing, *Gang*-like consequent.

Allegro con brio

Example 4.15

The above *Satz* appears first; it could count as an antecedent phrase, if only it were followed by a consequent instead of its own repetition a second lower (on B♭). This then leads to F (first major, then minor), and the whole is concluded, as an antecedent phrase, in the following manner: {255}

Example 4.16

At this point, the first *Satz* (Example 4.15) returns as – one must assume – a consequent phrase, with a change that need not concern us here. This latter phrase is also repeated, not on the second below but now on the second above, D, and a further modulation immediately follows, leading to the subsidiary *Satz*.

Similarly formed but even further worked out and thus more consequentially, more inwardly, of a piece, is the main *Satz* of Beethoven's immortal F minor Sonata, Op. 57. This is one of those works in which the spirit of the artist, completely imbued with its purposed task, reveals as inseparably united that which the ignorant often regard as irreconcilable opposites: the freest flight of creative power and the most profound logic and rationality.[7] The investigation of this *Satz* may be left, without further ado, to those who would study further.

From the enlarged period, which presents several *Sätze* combined within its form, it is but a step to the last form that the main *Satz* of a sonata is accustomed to take, one which indeed boasts the richest content and is the most characteristic, when compared to the main *Satz* of the rondo forms.

---

[7] [Marx:] Beethoven has long enough been taxed with eccentricity, and a detachment from form, if not with extravagance or deviant formlessness, while at the same time credited with fantasy and genius – and this from cultivated specialists who are not willing to step beyond a comfortably backward point, as well as from those magpie aestheticians, reviewers, etc., who hide their lack of cultivation behind technical phrasemaking. A more profound understanding of the essence of form would have shown that it is precisely Beethoven who, next to and alongside Sebastian Bach, demonstrates in his works the most energetic creation of form, i.e. the deepest logic and rationality – deeper than is mostly the case with Mozart, to whom it is customary, by way of an inherited habit imbibed in our youth, to accord a completely indefensible advantage in this respect as well.

The *Satz*-chain

The *Satz*-chain is a succession of *Sätze* that indeed belong to each other by dint of mood, the ordering of harmonic progressions, linking and mediating members, and common motives, but are not fused into a necessary unity through the firmly uniting periodic form.

Here we must think above all of that case already discussed in {256} Examples 4.2 to 4.4. The final *Satz* is related to the first but can also subsist independently without it.

Beethoven's G major Sonata, Op. 31 [No. 1], born of tenderness and sparkling caprice, gives a more decisive example. At first an antecedent phrase seems to form (see Example 4.1, p. 95 [in "Sonata form"]), only quite extended, with a full cadence on the dominant instead of the half cadence, and assembled from two different motives. Before anything else happens, the first three subsections are now repeated a step lower, on F, but then the main motive (a in Example 4.1, p. 95) is led from the six-four harmony on C to a full cadence on C, and then from the six-four harmony on G to a full cadence on G, so that the entire main *Satz* consists of fourteen subsections within thirty bars. And even with this, as we shall see presently, the main *Satz* has not yet exhausted its sway.

In this example, the individual subsections were in part so insignificant (namely in and of themselves) that one was compelled to recognize that the composer's idea was not to be grasped in the subsections but in the whole; each individual subsection by itself was only valid as a feature of the whole. We see the opposite case in the thoughtful main *Satz* of Beethoven's Op. 28 Sonata. Here is the first *Satz* (resting on a pedal point), self-sufficient and closed:

Example 4.17

It is repeated in a higher octave; then a second, and similar, *Satz* follows:

Example 4.18

After the transition that takes flight in its last few bars, this too is re-peated in a higher octave and closed in the tonic key.

Here the second *Satz* enjoys a clearly pronounced relation with the first. Let Mozart's graceful F major Sonata [K. 332][8] serve as an example of a looser concatenation, {257} in which the variety of content and the abundance of every *Satz* bring together that which each of the previous cases demonstrated only partially. The sonata begins with this *Satz*:

Example 4.19

Regardless of the completely foreign content of its second half and a half cadence whose form is made indistinct by the pedal point, this *Satz* can pass for a period, and it comes to a full cadence in the tonic at bar 12. At this point (since the periodic form leads no further), a completely different idea follows, a *Satz*:

Example 4.20

[8] [Marx:] In the first vol. of the B&H collected works.

This repeats, with an inessential alteration, and makes a full cadence once again in the tonic, which cadence is then repeated two more times. Now, whether one acknowledges the first idea (Example 4.19) as a period or as a *Satz* that only resembles a period, it cannot be disputed that a new *Satz* comes after it and that the main *Satz* thus combines two or three completely different ideas. That the last *Satz* (Example 4.20) belongs to the main *Satz*, regardless of the full close that precedes it, is shown at first by the identity of key and still more decisively by the further course of the composition, which we will consider later.[9] Yet the designation *main Satz* seems neither reasonable nor applicable here; the designation *main group* [*Hauptpartie*] would more appropriately epitomize everything up to the subsidiary *Satz*, or the *subsidiary group* [*Seitenpartie*].

Beethoven advances still more freely in his D major Sonata, Op. 10. He first brings on a period with extended consequent phrase: {258}

Example 4.21

The consequent phrase is repeated – with a light figuration, as indicated at a:

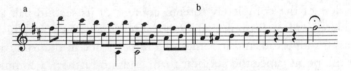

Example 4.22

Then the antecedent phrase is repeated as well, up to its fourth bar, whereupon, as b in Example 4.22 shows, it too is continued with inessential changes. Only after the half cadence on the dominant of B (at b) does a new idea appear, one that is completely foreign to the first in terms of key center and content:

---

[9] See below, 129–30.

Example 4.23

This is a period in B minor that cadences on its dominant; regardless of this unusual cadence, in the dominant instead of the relative major, this should be viewed as the first part of a songlike *Satz*. The second part does not lead back to the first, in fact it does not close at all, but rather flows out into a *Gang* that brings us over A major and F♯ minor to E major (dominant of the dominant) and from there to A major. At this point there is a full and formal close, and only then is the subsidiary *Satz* in A major introduced, itself a formally constructed period whose repetition then leads further afield.

It would be easy, but superfluous, to multiply such examples or to introduce those featuring still more manifold combinations (one should examine the main *Satz* of Beethoven's grand B♭ major Sonata, Op. 106, or C.M. Weber's A♭ major Sonata). As in the previous cases, we would everywhere come across the characteristic features of sonata form, already evident here in the main *Satz*: enhanced motion, and a richer content that is to be adhered to amid constant metamorphosis. Whenever this {259} mobility could become checked, through a sharply closed *Satz*-form or periodic form, either a new *Satz* must appear (which then yields the *Satz*-chain) or the strict periodic form must be opened up (yielding the enlarged period or the *Gang*-like continuation of the consequent phrase), or the *Satz* must be repeated and then led further. If not, the character of sonata form will be compromised – another form should have been chosen.

Let us now observe the further sway of this driving impulse, so native to the sonata.

SECTION TWO: PROGRESSION TO THE SUBSIDIARY *SATZ*

If we are to protect ourselves from hasty and one-sided judgements or rules, then we must steadily keep in mind how greatly varied the content of sonata form has already proved to be, even in the few main *Sätze* that we considered in the preceding section. We have already seen main groups consisting of *Sätze*, periods, and successions of related and different *Sätze*; in [our treatment of] orchestral composition, we shall add a variety of polyphonic main *Sätze*. None of these different types is dispensable, none absolutely preferred. But *each desires to be continued in a manner suited to its nature.*

This principle – the only justifiable law – is of itself manifest and needs no further discussion; it is the same principle that has been our constant and ubiquitous guide. Nonetheless, its application needs to be considered with all the more care, since this is chiefly a question of comprehending the content of every single piece of music.

The formation of the main *Satz* is the first product of the Idea, the mood – in short, of the motivation for the composition that is to come into being. It determines all that follows.

It *first* determines that the composition thus begun should indeed assume sonata form. A quick perusal of the main *Sätze* imparted in the previous section and elsewhere will at the least place beyond doubt the fact that none of them could subsist as a *Liedsatz*[10] or would be suitable as the main *Satz* for a rondo of the first through fourth forms. Would they not be suitable for a rondo of the fifth form? This can be a tricky question with several of the main *Sätze*, because this rondo type forms the transition to sonata form, and, as is well known, at such points of transition the borders of each form flow into each other. But the more a main *Satz* is formed in the manner of a sonata (we have in mind those on pp. 109–15), {**260**} i.e. the more resolutely it distances itself from the song form and from the general manner of the rondo, the less it will seem suited even to the fifth rondo form.

Next, the formation of the main *Satz* also determines the way one must progress from it to the subsidiary *Satz*. One may choose from among various ways of continuing; but this choice is not entrusted to arbitrary caprice (which, as we have seen, is generally excluded from the essence of art) but rather is determined in accordance with reason, from the content and essence of the whole, and initially of the main *Satz*, which is all that yet exists of the future whole.

In particular, we can distinguish three ways of making this transition; we now need to consider them in turn.

---

[10] For this term, see "Form in music" (pp. 72–73 above).

Continuation of the last member of the main *Satz*

This manner of proceeding from the main *Satz* must *in general* be deemed the most available and consequential; it forms a direct and forward-moving progression both from and out of the idea last presented. Yet, in order that it may satisfy the dictates of reason, it must be just as grounded in the content and formation of the main *Satz* as we shall find is the case with the other ways of proceeding.

In what case can – or must – we now progress directly from the last member of the main *Satz*?

In those instances where the formation of the main *Satz* shows it to be incomplete in itself and in need of continuation. This is chiefly the case with the period with incomplete or open consequent (presented above, starting on p. 107).

The finale of Beethoven's C♯ minor Sonata exhibited a broadly laid out antecedent phrase as its main *Satz* (Example 4.13). This antecedent phrase demands its consequent. And one indeed follows, entering with the first two bars of the antecedent phrase. Yet the entire content, the arpeggiating motive, has already been sufficiently portrayed; after the abundant antecedent phrase, the consequent is no longer required for the sake of its content but for the sake of the form, which is conditioned by the antecedent's harmonic progression and half cadence. Hence the consequent phrase is immediately opened up; after the repetition of those first two bars, the same motive is repeated in the first two bars of the following example:

Example 4.24

{261} With these two chords (or, better, already with the first chord), the appointed key of the subsidiary *Satz*, G♯ minor, is reached; the subsidiary *Satz* appears without further ado in the bars that follow.

It was possible to proceed with such torrential swiftness here because the essential content of the main *Satz*, namely the main motive, was already of a *Gang*-like nature and, as mentioned above, had already been sufficiently executed. The big C major Sonata (the antecedent phrase of its main *Satz* was given in Examples 4.15 and 4.16) behaves similarly. After the cadence of the antecedent phrase (Example 4.16), the first section (Example 4.15) returns (as mentioned already on p. 111) and is repeated a step higher. Then there is a further modulation using the last motive, over B to E:

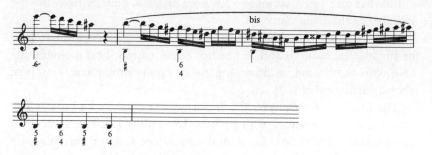

Example 4.25

After another six bars, resting on the dominant of E, the subsidiary *Satz* enters in that key. It is almost the exact same case as the previous example, only that the dominant of the dominant is at least touched upon here, and then, however, a transition is fashioned completely in the manner of a pedal point. Here too the core (Example 4.15) of the main *Satz* is sufficiently presented – four times – and the transition (Example 4.25) motivated by the similar cadential turn of the antecedent phrase (Example 4.16).

The small F minor Sonata, presented in Example 4.11, is even more succinct. The parallel key, in which the subsidiary *Satz* will appear, is already reached in the fifth bar of the consequent phrase (Example 4.12); a lightly conceived appendix (after Example 4.12) reinforces the modulation, in that it twice touches on the dominant (the last two bars are repeated):

Example 4.26

And now the subsidiary *Satz* enters, its first moment even in the key of the dominant.[11] An identical manner of transition, only executed in grander proportions, can be observed in the large F minor Sonata, Op. 57.

The sonata presented on p. 114 [Op. 10, No. 3, in D] offers us the last example in this series. As we know, after a period whose consequent, {262} and then its antecedent, were repeated (Example 4.22), an entirely new *Satz* appeared in B minor (Example 4.23), in form not unlike the first part of a song [form] and with a cadence in F♯ minor. A second part now seems to want to form from the motives of this new *Satz* (or it at least alludes to those motives):

Example 4.27

Yet, after its first section in A major has been repeated, the *Satz* opens out in the manner of a *Gang*:

Example 4.28

This leads over A major, F♯ minor, and E major to A major and the subsidiary *Satz*.

If we summarize all the cases presented here and otherwise belonging here, this is the result: this readily available progression, from the last sounded idea of the main *Satz*, succeeds either if that idea is the only essential idea of the main *Satz*, or if a preceding *Satz* has been dispatched sufficiently. If the latter is not the case, if the composer has aroused an idea and left it insufficiently presented, then the following category of continuation is motivated.

---

[11] Such a claim makes clear the distance between our own and Marx's view of modulation and the establishment of keys. We would be much more likely to view the entrance of the subsidiary *Satz* as being on the dominant harmony and not actually in the dominant key.

Return to an earlier idea

This earlier idea is thus designated as the main motive of the main *Satz*.

We can observe this sufficiently enough in the Sonatas in E♭ and G by Beethoven, mentioned above [on pp. 103 and 95]. After the first idea of the E♭ Sonata (Example 4.2) a second idea (Example 4.4) has emerged from the main motive of the first and been repeated. From here a *Gang* forms in the already attained key of B♭, and seems to want to lead to the subsidiary *Satz*.

Example 4.29

But the first and most distinguished idea has been too soon suppressed by the second (which is so subordinate that we legitimately called it a mere appendix above [on p. 104]). One must come back to it, and only now – with its second and most expansive motive – is it led to the dominant of the dominant {263} and to the subsidiary *Satz*.

Example 4.30

(The second and third bis are performed up an octave.)

Even more telling is the next example, from the G major Sonata. The core [*Kern*] of the main *Satz*, with its most distinct motive (a), is given in Example 4.1 [in "Sonata form," p. 95]. It is faithfully replicated a step lower, i.e. in F, and closes in C, just as before it had closed in D. This cadential formula is then repeated twice with the main motive a, or rather with its last four-bar subsection:

Example 4.31

And then, in recall of the first motive (bar 1 in Example 4.1), a *Gang* drives forth precipitately, coming to rest, after fourteen bars, on a half cadence.

Example 4.32

This move was made doubly necessary by the motive of the first bar and by the fragmentary nature of all that followed. And yet, while this is going on, the main motive a is suppressed, and an element of haste is introduced into the composition that does not accord with its primary content and cannot be allowed to predominate. Consequently: Beethoven returns to his opening, thus proceeding from that surprising move [the long *Gang*] to the motive that prepared and engendered it (bar 1 in Example 4.1) and from there, pursuing his core *Satz* still further, to the steadier main motive. In its eighth bar, however, [the *Satz*] turns to (B and) F♯ major, instead of to D, as was the case in the opening:

Example 4.33

{264} This turn is confirmed by repeating the whole [of the above example] once and repeating its cadential bars twice. After a decorated extension of the cadential tonic [see Example 4.34], the subsidiary *Satz* enters in B major.

Example 4.34

—For the disciple of art as for the merely observing yet thoughtful friend of art, this entire main group (along with the unsettling key of the subsidiary *Satz*) offers especially instructive testimony to the conviction, so often expressed here, that there is no caprice in the true artwork but only reasoned freedom. The entire group can easily give the impression, at a first and tentative hearing, of an almost incoherent gush of sound, tossed off by arbitrary caprice. At the very outset, the second motive (a) does not at all follow from the first motive; it stands, in fact, as its exact contradiction. But a deeper investigation reveals with ever more illumination the logic of the whole. That driving first motive, taking flight with unbounded spirits, like a sudden inspiration, could call forth a *Gang* (which indeed happens later) but not a *Satz*. Thus it must come to a standstill, as if in contemplation; it must be followed, or rather faced with, that second motive (a). Only this latter can be intensified and then rounded off as a *Satz*. But now the first motive has been supplanted and, at the same time, the key of the dominant has been reached prematurely (as indeed befits the precipitate sense of the whole). Consequently, the first motive returns, and then the second again after it. Had this taken place back in G or in its dominant D, already alluded to, it would not have corresponded to the flighty character of the whole; thus the harmony leaps into F (any formal transition would have been too ponderous for the flighty and fragmentary nature of this *Satz*). But now the second motive (on account of the necessity of returning to the tonic key) is granted a still greater ascendancy over the first motive. The composer has become ... an even greater debtor to that motive; he must finally indulge it, and it then brings forth (Example 4.32) what it can: a *Gang*, and indeed a highly precipitate one, fully in character. And should this *Gang* be allowed to hurry off to the subsidiary *Satz*?— If so, then our stalwart motive (a) would fall out of mind, and the entire main group would lose its backbone. Then should the main motive return immediately?— It would no longer be motivated, as it was at the beginning, since the other motive has just completed itself.[12] It obviously needs some mediation, and this is provided by the return of the very opening, {265} from which had emerged both that *Gang* as well as, earlier on, the necessary appearance of the (a) motive. With this it also

---

[12] I.e. the main motive was motivated at the beginning of the movement by the way the initial *Gang*-like motive was cut off; thus the completely realized *Gang* we have just heard cannot serve to motivate the return of the main motive.

became necessary to effect the transition to the subsidiary *Satz* not by that *Gang*, but by the *Satz*-like component of the main group. The need for a *Gang*-like bridging passage (*Satz* to *Satz* makes no such link) is satisfied at the last moment by that mediating figure from Example 4.34. —We shall return later to the subsidiary *Satz* and its key center.

Similar cases, to be understood in the same manner, can be seen in Beethoven's *Pathétique* Sonata (Example 4.5), in Mozart's C minor Sonata (with its preceding fantasia), and in many other compositions. The Mozartian sonata at first presents a periodic main *Satz*:

Example 4.35

Both its cadences are incomplete (the half cadence falls on a diminished seventh chord) and therefore urge further progress. Yet both of the period's motives have been sufficiently presented for the nonce; thus a new *Satz* appears, with this beginning:

Example 4.36

It repeats, with upper voices inverted, and continues on with completely different motives:

Example 4.37

But the main idea may not be given up, especially not if it is to be supplanted by an idea weaker in content and form. Consequently the former returns again and leads, with a shock, to the subsidiary *Satz*. After the repetition of the first two bars {266} of Example 4.35, the bass seizes the main motive and the upper voice counterpoints it:

Example 4.38

In the following bar, the subsidiary *Satz* makes its appearance in E♭. — Here again the dominant key (B♭) of the new key center has been avoided; we will observe the consequences of this in the next section.[13]

We find a common feature in all these examples: a decisively terse drive to the subsidiary *Satz*, just as soon as the main *Satz* has been settled. Thus that which is once determined to be essential clearly comes to the fore here: namely, main *Satz* and subsidiary *Satz*. The merely mediating parts must limit themselves, as befits their subordinate significance; yet they too readily assume *Satz* form (as far as their natures will allow) and in both respects attest to the energy and thorough overview of their creator [*Bildner*].

In conclusion, let us take another look at the Dussek Sonata from Example 4.7. The main *Satz*, a period, allowed no continuation; its appendix, or second *Satz* (Example 4.8), also seemed not to want to continue, but at least managed to suppress the real main *Satz*. Thus this latter

[13] See below, pp. 145–46.

must return, and it presumably becomes more mobile through a lively counterpoint or continuo part (the bass sounds an octave lower than written here).

Example 4.39

Yet such mobility is not attainable through externally applied figuration, but only through inner construction, through the essential nature of the *Satz* – and the *Satz* has here remained unchanged, just as immobile as before. At least the periodic form is done away with; the passage closes in the dominant in the fourth bar.

Thus a relatively new *Satz* is formed; however, only through its hasty close in the dominant has it surpassed the period in Example 4.7 in terms of having some power to progress. This new *Satz* demands a confirming repetition; the form demands progress. Thus it is repeated in B♭ {267} with a close on F (while the counterpoint is transferred to the upper voice), and then repeated a third time in F major (with counterpoint again appearing in the bass). This manner of progressing, where each successive stage is reached in the same way and then traveled over again (this indicates the use of *Satz*-form), does not so much advance as get *shoved* ahead.

The composer feels this and, in the last repetition, opens the *Satz* up from the third bar on in the manner of a *Gang*:

Example 4.40

With the last half of the fourth bar, this returns once again to the main key and the transitional *Satz* (Example 4.39), which is finally led to F, where the first theme group closes in the manner of a pedal point.

Thus we have before us a main *Satz* of *eight* bars – or *fourteen*, counting the appended *Satz* – after which a group of *twenty-five* bars is required for the transition to the second-theme group: only the *eight* bars of the period are in fact essential; the remaining *thirty-eight* bars are mere accessories.

Why did the composer return again to the *Satz* in E♭ major after the first *Gang* (Example 4.40), instead of immediately confirming the dominant of the dominant with a readily available move such as the following (fashioned after Example 4.40)?

Example 4.41

Clearly he did so only because he himself felt that the uniform and inanimate manner in which he shoved along to F, from dominant to dominant, *Satz* after *Satz*, was not satisfactory, was not sufficiently *Gang*-like and impulsively decisive. Whether or not he would have arrived more freshly at his goal by using a passage like the one in Example 4.41 than by returning to the main key and attaching a second *Gang* to a goal that had already been reached is a question we need not dwell on, because this same composer has shown himself so abundantly accomplished in musical forms. But precisely for this reason, {**268**} the fundamental cause of these weaknesses, which are so manifest here and so difficult to discount, is all the more apparent. First a main *Satz* was presented that, on account of its form, was perforce relieved of its power to continue further. Then there was a failure to grasp means suitably energetic for the required continuation; the section intended to be mobile proved stagnant once again. Finally, thus checked yet again by this material, the composer lost the correct point of view for the proper valuation of main and subsidiary matter; he gave the latter the same space, in fact much more than the same space, quite overbalancing the former.

It could easily be shown that all those composers who attend to their tasks with less energy, who follow external rather than inwardly profound motivations, are guilty of this same favoritism toward subsidiary material – toward transitional sections; this is apparent not only among all the so-called virtuoso composers or salon composers (who write on behalf of one particular instrument or manner of playing, or for the sake of bravura and fashion) but also among the masters, whenever they – as a matter of exception – comply with such external aims, as for instance in concerted works. I will have more to say about this in the fourth volume of this method, on the occasion of concerto composition; thus there is even less need for a more detailed discussion here.

It has occasionally come to our attention here that the main *Satz* does not always offer likely material for continuation. This leads us to the third manner of transition.

Progression to the subsidiary *Satz* by means of new motives

The sonata presented in Examples 4.9 and 4.10 [Op. 2, No. 3] provides the first case of this type. Both the period, which was made to act as main *Satz*, and the *Satz* derived from it, along with its repetition, progress with a series of terse jolts. One *could* use the same motives – such a thing would be possible with *any Satz* – moving forward from, say, the repetition of Example 4.10 through D and G to the subsidiary *Satz*.

Example 4.42

But wouldn't this use up the facile main motive, which we have already heard, in all its abruptness, four times in a row? And how much time would we need in order to bring these succinct, always so distinctly isolated members {269} into an animated flow, all the more desirable after such an opening?—

Beethoven, always with the right feel for the entire state of affairs, tears himself away from his main *Satz* and attaches a completely new *Gang*-like *Satz* to its final tone:

Example 4.43

This is repeated, starting in the very next bar, but then immediately led (in the third subsequent bar) over A minor and D major to G major. A *Satz* that lingers on G in the manner of a pedal point serves to reinforce this key and to round off and conclude the main group decisively:

Example 4.44

It is then repeated and closed with a one-bar scalar descent of sixteenth notes. The result is an appended half cadence in the manner of the sonatina, a final cadence, as it were, for the main group. The subsidiary *Satz* follows immediately.

The similarity of this case with the previous one is unmistakable.[14] Here too we have a period and an added *Satz*, neither of which wanted continuation. Beethoven not only recognizes this but just as clearly realizes what his main *Satz* lacks in terms of mobility (or flow) and verve; with one fell swoop he provides what is lacking and, after the thirteen bars of the main idea, reaches his goal in another fourteen bars (the thirteenth bar of the main *Satz* and the first bar of the transitional *Satz* are elided). Dussek also realizes the degree to which his main idea lacks the mobility to press on ahead; but he would make good this lack with cosmetic accessories [*Beiwerk*], an added contrapuntal line which of course essentially changes nothing. The *Satz* in Example 4.39 has as little impetus to move forward as that of Example 4.7; in the main (apart from the difference between *Satz* and period) they are the same.

A second example is offered by the Mozartian sonata to whose first two *Sätze* (of the first-theme group) we were introduced in Examples 4.19 and 4.20.

{270} The first of these (the period) could lead no further. Had one wanted to carry it forth, one would have had to extend the consequent phrase and lead it to the dominant (thus building a first part); then one would have had to return to the antecedent phrase and finally (since this phrase is less mobile) touch once again upon the consequent phrase. Doing so will have given the whole idea, whose significance does not equal its grace and charm, much too much space – and no livelier progression will have been attained anyway, due to the lack of an appropriate motive.

Even the second *Satz* (Example 4.20), though livelier than the first, does not yield a sufficiently fresh sense of progress. Before anything else, its first subsection needs to be repeated, which Mozart does. But instead of staying in the same place, it would have to be able to move elsewhere, e.g. up a step and in minor:

Example 4.45

[14] Marx is referring to the Dussek example which closed the last section (see pp. 124–27 above).

(Here the more animated motive a, which enters a bar earlier in the Mozart, has to be delayed so that the move to another key could be mitigated by the closer motivic connection.) And then it would have to be carried out some way or another as a *Gang* to the dominant:

Example 4.46

Yet even here Mozart's agreeable invention would become undeservedly broad, and the easy flow of the whole would be lost; not to mention the fact that Mozart was in any event more inclined to a delicately fluttering manner.[15]

Like Beethoven, the master hits upon the only solution. He abandons both the second *Satz* and the first and forms a third, *Gang*-like *Satz*:

Example 4.47

He repeats this with a turn toward C minor and then increases the animation of its main motive: {**271**}

Example 4.48

With this he gets to C minor, ending the main group with a half cadence on its dominant. After *two* additional *Sätze*, Mozart has here achieved the same thing as Beethoven in the preceding example.

Similar cases, as, for example, the sonata in Example 4.14, can be left to one's own consideration; we will return to that sonata for other rea-

---

[15] Note how Marx's proposed alteration would give the passage a somewhat Beethovenian thrust. In dismissing it, he recognizes how foreign this would be to Mozart's sensibility.

sons in Example 4.58. But let us cast our final glance here at Beethoven's colossal B♭ major Sonata, Op. 106. As is the case throughout, this masterwork already presents an entire series of profound and powerful ideas as its main group.

Example 4.49

After the galvanic upward thrust of this introduction, the first fully realized idea of the main group appears as a period with the following antecedent phrase:

Example 4.50

At the conclusion of this period a new *Satz* (a) appears:

Example 4.51

Repeated four times with rising intensity (on the pedal point [b]), it then jolts forth to a half cadence on the dominant. It goes without saying that the half cadence cannot suffice after such a powerful beginning and for such a wealth of ideas; nor can the beginning (Example 4.49), at this point only a sketch, remain without echo or continuation. It indeed returns, but its ultimate strokes seize upon the harmony d–f♯–a (standing for d–f♯–a–c),[16] thus attaining the key of the subsidiary *Satz*, G

---

[16] This is my reading of "statt d–fis–a–c": to translate "statt" as "instead" gives the impression that what would have been expected there is a D⁷ chord and that Beethoven fools us with the mere triad.

major, with a boldly overreaching grasp. If one considers that the preceding *Sätze* were very rich harmonically (much more so than is indicated in Examples 4.50 and 4.51) and that {272} this bold reach into the new key is thoroughly in character with the whole, then one understands that no further mediation or reinforcement of the new key through its dominant is needed, that such a ceremonious and circumlocutionary modulation could only sap the power of the whole. Thus Beethoven treats the new key as a *fait accompli* but, before the subsidiary *Satz* follows, makes us feel at home there with a broadly executed, *Gang*-like pedal point, which draws on the main motive of Example 4.49. The introduction has *four* bars, the period *thirteen*, the *Gang*-like *Satz eighteen* (of which the first bar is elided with the previous cadence), the introductory idea another *four*, and the pedal point *twenty-five* bars, on the last of which the subsidiary *Satz* begins. Thus there are *twenty-five* bars of transition (or, rather, of confirmation of the already accomplished transition) as against the *thirty-eight* bars that belong to the essential *Sätze*.

SECTION THREE: THE FURTHER COURSE OF THE FIRST PART

What we have already learned about the main *Satz* goes for the subsidiary *Satz* as well: it can take the form of the *Satz*, period, or even the two-part song form, or it can present a series of *Sätze*. Its formation, as well as the entire further development of the First Part, steadfastly follows the law given by the formation of the main *Satz* and by the further course of the main group. We may thus take a summary view of this whole second block of the First Part and limit ourselves primarily to a consideration of such examples as make visible this logical development and the different directions it takes.

And yet the formation of the subsidiary *Satz* does not follow mechanically from that of the main group: e.g. if the main *Satz* is a period then the subsidiary *Satz* must be a period, etc. Rather the subsidiary *Satz* must complete (for the First Part) what the main *Satz* has begun, but only *in the same sense*; it must supplement what the latter has, for whatever reason, left unfulfilled – and this not only *can* but often *must* take place with forms entirely different from those of the main *Satz*.

In general, we know the following about the subsidiary *Satz*: {273}

First. It must form a whole with the main *Satz*, internally through mood and externally through its key area and use of the same meter (these latter not without exceptions); consequently it must preserve a certain unity and concord.

Second. At the same time, however, it must disengage itself decisively from the main *Satz* through its content, namely through its harmonic progression[17] and also through its form, establishing itself as something other, as an antithesis; main *Satz* and subsidiary *Satz* face each other as antitheses that are intimately joined within a comprehensive whole, forming a higher unity.

Third. In this pair of themes, the main *Satz* is the first to be determined, thus partaking of an initial freshness and energy, and as such is the more energetic, pithy, and unconditional formation, that which leads and determines. The subsidiary *Satz*, on the other hand, is created after the first energetic confirmation and, by contrast, is that which serves. It is conditioned and determined by the preceding theme, and as such its essence is necessarily milder, its formation one of pliancy rather than pith – a feminine counterpart, as it were, to its masculine precedent. In just such a sense, each theme is a thing apart until both together form a higher, more perfected entity.[18]

Fourth. In this sense, however, and true to the general tendency of sonata form, it has also been established that both themes have the same warrant, that the subsidiary *Satz* is not just peripheral business, not just a secondary theme to the main theme, and thus claims, in general, the same development and the same space as the main theme; whereby there can of course be no question of a small-minded practice of counting measures.—

---

[17] Marx uses the word *Modulation* here, which should not be confused with change of key. Like other theorists of the early nineteenth century, Marx employed this word generally to denote harmonic progression; he would often mark an actual change of key with the phrase "modulation to another key," or with the words *Ausweichung* or *Übergang* (although, confusingly enough, he also used the word *Modulation* at times to denote the general business of changing key). In the first thesis he mentions the *Sitz seiner Modulation*, referring to the key center of the second theme's harmonic progression. Translating both these instances with our word "modulation" would be to assert that Marx, in this thesis, thinks of the modulation to the second theme as a sign of unity, while in the next thesis he regards it as a sign of contrast.

[18] This passage, suggesting the masculine nature of the main *Satz* and the feminine nature of the subsidiary *Satz*, has recently been the subject of much scrutiny. See Susan McClary, *Feminine Endings: Music, Gender, and Sexuality* (Minneapolis: University of Minnesota Press, 1991), 13; Marcia Citron, *Gender and the Musical Canon* (Cambridge: Cambridge University Press, 1993), 132–35; James Hepokoski, "Masculine–feminine," *Musical Times* 135 (August 1994), 494–99; and Scott Burnham, "A. B. Marx and the gendering of sonata form," in *Music Theory in the Age of Romanticism*, ed. Ian Bent (Cambridge: Cambridge University Press, 1996), 163–86.

As we know, that which now follows the subsidiary *Satz* (*Gang* and closing *Satz*) can only be the result of either the subsidiary *Satz* or the main *Satz*.

Supported by these already familiar fundamental precepts, let us now proceed without further ado to the illumination of individual cases, which we will order according to the forms available to the subsidiary *Satz*.

Satz-form

In Beethoven's E♭ major Sonata (Example 4.2) we found the main group developed with sufficient variety, despite the persistence of the main motive. After an initial *Satz*, a second *Satz* formed (Example 4.4), both variable upon repetition; after a new *Satz*-like *Gang* (Example 4.29) the first idea returned completely transformed (Example 4.30). All these *Sätze*, and especially the main idea, moved in sections and limbs that were quick to break off. How, then, is the subsidiary group shaped?

As it must be in order to carry on and complete the main group. {274} Above all, the subsidiary *Satz* sounds more intimately cohesive and flowing (admittedly with the aid of its accompaniment but also through it essential content), and does so in order to bring to the whole more firmness and flow after the fragmented main *Sätze*.

Example 4.52

After a freely imagined four-bar run (which, like the third bar of the above example, is lightly reminiscent of the main group),[19] this subsidi-

---

[19] To clarify here: the third bar of Example 4.52 probably reminds Marx of bars 20 and 24; the four-bar "run" (bars 53–56) reminds him of bars 25 and 27.

ary *Satz* is repeated with even more animation, and a closing *Satz* (which is repeated up an octave) seems to want to form already:

Example 4.53

But even though this opposition of subsidiary group to main group certainly bodes well for the whole, the steady hand of our composer cannot let the main group simply slip from his grasp. He leads away from this presumed closing *Satz* with a *Gang*, pulling in motives from the *Gang* in the main group (Example 4.29), and then builds his closing *Satz*, not without a faint allusion (bars 2 and 3 below) to the main motive.

Example 4.54

—Thus main and subsidiary groups belong to each other not merely through the prevailing mood of the whole, their closely related keys, and their metrical identity, but even through shared or recalled motives – and yet they stand opposed in such a way that the one side is granted that which had to remain denied to the other.

We can observe this as well in the smaller proportions of the sonata from Example 4.11 [Op. 2, No. 1]. The main *Satz* is built from two-bar sections that thrust upwards; the subsidiary *Satz* answers this almost word for word through a downwardly turned motive: {275}

Example 4.55

This flows on, by means of a coherent and uniform accompaniment (which the main *Satz* did not have), and is repeated three times, the third time leading into a beautifully vaulting *Gang* that is equally mobile, until the closing *Satz*, itself repeated three times, returns to the type of motion and accompaniment of the main *Satz*.

The same thing could be shown in the G major sonata referred to in Example 4.1 [in "Sonata form," p. 95]; here, however, we are chiefly concerned with the point of modulation. The subsidiary *Satz* does not enter in D major – but in B major. In terms of the series of major key relations [i.e. the circle of fifths], this would be *four* keys away from D; if one takes the relative minor of D and then changes it to major, then it is *three* keys away. What is behind this significant deviation from the fundamental law of modulation ...?

This question – and all similar questions – cannot be unequivocally answered here. For the judgement of every individual composition involves not only the general laws and conditions of its form but also the specific content, Idea, mood, etc. of just this specific work; in the same manner, the judgement of an individual human being and his or her actions involve not only general circumstances, nationality, age, gender, class, and so forth, but also the essence and particular circumstances of just this specific person. Nevertheless, those general circumstances (as we have seen many times before in other cases) already throw sufficient light on this case to allow us to realize that here too deviation from a fundamental law happens not out of caprice but for reasons that reside in the matter itself.

As was the case with our first example (Op. 31, [No.] 3) – and to an even greater degree, since the main *Satz* of the present example is broken up more frequently and with shorter fragments – Beethoven here needs a firmer and more continuously formed subsidiary *Satz* that would be capable of giving the whole the necessary element of stability [*Haltung*] and that is thus of especial importance. In what key could he have placed his subsidiary *Satz*?

In the dominant, D major? But this has been so strongly impressed – already at the very outset (Example 4.1) with a formal transition, and then with that powerfully engaging *Gang* (Example 4.32) whose final chord [D] is broadly arpeggiated through six bars and then decisively closed as a half cadence – that returning to it yet again would lack all freshness and energy.

Since the key of D must now be refused the next choice was its relative minor: {276} B minor. Yet the capriciously cheerful, sparkling, and vivacious character of this sonata, namely of the preceding main

Satz, could never countenance the gloomy minor mode; consequently, it is transformed into major.

Now let us observe the further influence of this migration over D major and B minor to B major. The latter key appeared of necessity, but B minor was closer and D major closest of all; this hierarchy could not remain without influence. The subsidiary *Satz* is thus first presented in B major and repeated with a firmer cadential formulation.

Example 4.56

Then, as if in remorse over the passed-over keys, the same *Satz* enters in (!) B minor (with melody in the bass and sixteenth-note accompaniment); upon repetition it turns to (!) D major. From here the music goes further, following F♯, E, and D to a cadence in B minor, moves again to D and then through the same course reaches another cadence in B minor. This is followed by the diminutive closing *Satz* in B minor, which is compelled, however, to remember again the B major that was at first so necessary and then so yielding.

Example 4.57

In this way the initial urge to major (B major) has indeed been satisfied and not forgotten, while the more closely related minor key has maintained its right and the closest key, D major, has been touched upon three times, thus receiving as much compensatory exposure as was its due under such circumstances. Enticingly fresh, the key of B major has reached our ears like the sound of graceful song from a distant land. Without impairing the increased cohesiveness so necessary to the second theme, the change of key here is stimulating enough to correspond entirely to the tricksy mischief of the main group.[20]

---

[20] In a footnote at this point, Marx refers the reader to an appendix on form and modulation, in which he invokes Mozart's oft-cited letter about key relations in *Die Entführung aus dem Serail*.

To conclude this series of examples, we introduce two cases in which the subsidiary *Satz*, out of respect for the main group, has had to abstain from a more significant development.

The first of these is offered by the Beethovenian sonata from Example 4.14 (Op. 90 in E minor), one of the most thoughtfully profound creations (at least in its first movement) that has been granted us in all of music. In its first movement there is not a single feature that could not claim to be the unmediated {277} and purest expression of a deeply moved spirit. As an expanded period, the main *Satz* is richly fashioned even to the point of utter satiation, full of emphatically affecting eloquence; then it closes itself off, leading no further. Thus a new *Satz* appears, which soon breaks free in the manner of a *Gang*:

Example 4.58

The *Gang*-like half of this is repeated in A minor and B♭ major, then the first half builds the chord a♯ (formerly b♭)–c♯–e–g. And then, with step after step of the most eloquent song, this new *Satz* moves through B to F♯ and from there directly back to B minor for the subsidiary *Satz*. It is easy to understand why the subsidiary *Satz* goes to the minor dominant instead of the relative major (G major). In minor-key constructions, the relative major is the normative first choice for modulation only because *as a rule* the content of these compositions neither demands nor accepts the deeper gloom of minor piled onto minor ... When, as here, the opposite is the case, the rule and its foundation fall away of themselves; in addition, C major (Example 4.58) and B♭ major make pronounced appearances here between the two minor keys.

Yet the subsidiary *Satz* itself, in relation to the main *Satz*, appears less

---

In this letter, Mozart explains why he modulates from F to A minor instead of F to D minor (which is analogous to Beethoven's modulation to the mediant instead of the submediant).

developed; it is hardly more than a reply to the first section of the main group's second *Satz* (Example 4.58):

Example 4.59

Nor is it more richly unfolded in its intensified repetition (starting in bar 7 above); the closing *Satz* (consisting of four bars, their repetition, and an appendix [*Anhang*]) begins directly at the cadence of this repetition. This is {278} not the place to talk about how emotionally piercing both *Sätze* are or how painfully they seem to die away; this content, as well as the tone poet's own motives, would have occasioned a further and more deeply penetrating discussion. And yet both these events should not and could not be allowed a greater range, because the more manly, dignified, and, conjointly, deeper element had impressed itself too firmly in the main group to let itself be outweighed by the passionate resignation of the subsidiary group.— In this case the main group has *fifty-four* bars, the subsidiary group *twenty-seven* bars. —Moreover, it is worth noting that this relation between main and subsidiary groups is repeated in the larger proportions of this sonata. The movement we have been discussing dominates the remaining movement, namely the tender, but inwardly languishing finale, just as powerfully as its main group dominates its subsidiary group. This could not have been otherwise.

One can observe the same thing in C. M. v. Weber's substantial A♭ major Sonata. The main group unfolds in such broad strokes (one *Satz* of *eleven* bars, a second of *eight*, a third, which brings on the transition, of *twenty-four*) that the subsidiary *Satz* is limited, after being prepared in two foregoing bars, to *two* bars, which are repeated – and this because it has found everything that could be said in the form of a *Satz* already more than sufficiently expressed; a uniform, or even similar, treatment would exceedingly overload the whole. But this would then grant far too little consideration to the issue of balance; even in its content the subsidiary *Satz* does not impart the rise in spirits so desirable after the noble but rather too overflowing sentimentality of the main group. For this reason, a broader, more buoyant passage (*Satz*-like at its outset) is added; after eighteen bars it leads to the conclusion, or, rather, to the return of the opening, from whence the music continues on into the Second Part by means of a motive borrowed from the first *Satz*. Closer examination is left to the reader.

Periodic form

We find a subsidiary *Satz* that is constructed in the manner of a period in the *Pathétique* Sonata. After the broadly formed *Sätze* of the main group (Example 4.5) there appears, as a counter- or subsidiary *Satz*, an equally substantial but less consequentially articulated period. Here too the friendly nature of the relative major would not have corresponded to the sense of the main *Satz*; indeed, if the subsidiary group was already meant to appear more lightly articulated, as a contrast to the broadly managed main *Satz*, then to appear in major to boot would certainly have had a trivial or feeble effect. Thus Beethoven proceeds, in the way described above (p. 136), over E♭ major to E♭ minor; here he presents his subsidiary *Satz*, which answers the darkly boisterous, upward-storming thrusts of his first idea with restless strains of lament. {279}

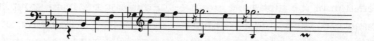

Example 4.60

But even here the key that is actually most closely related will not be forgotten; for now a second, urgently courageous, *Satz* (*Gang*-like and in place of a *Gang*) is formed in the very key of E♭ major and then repeated with a more emphatic close. The closing *Satz* is in E♭ major as well.

The big C major Sonata (Example 4.15) offers a similar case, in which the periodic formation of the subsidiary *Satz*, incidentally, appears less equivocally than in the above-mentioned composition. In light of the foregoing discussion, its modulation (the subsidiary *Satz* enters in E major) should be understood without difficulty.[21]

Subsidiary *Satz* as two-part song form

Through a whole series of cases, we have already come to appreciate the deep rationality in Beethoven's works (and in those of all true artists). This rationality expresses itself chiefly in that the whole [work] and each of its features are created out of the given Idea and stand in constant accordance with it. The other side of this highest characteristic of artistic nature is that it brings forth a genuine and consistent originality,[22] and thus the greatest variety among the collected works of an artist's œuvre, because each work is fashioned not according to some general rule of form or template,[23] but rather according to its own particular being.

And thus it is once again in the work of Beethoven, in his great B♭ major Sonata (Example 4.49), that we even find a two-part song form – or at least the onset of one – used as a subsidiary *Satz*. Here is its first part:

Example 4.61

It could, on account of its brevity, be taken for a mere antecedent phrase, but it contains within it the cadence of an antecedent phrase (in the second bar, or if one converts the example to simple 2/4, from the third to fourth bar)[24] and the formal end-of-section cadence in the key of the dominant. {280} The second part is then continued on and led to a

---

[21] The modulatory scheme of Op. 53 is in fact exactly analogous to that of Op. 31, No. 1.

[22] [Marx:] Genuine originality goes hand in hand with genuine fidelity; false originality seeks things that are allegedly new, surprising, and of great effect, things not grounded in the matter itself – it thus destroys the work and character of the artist that has fallen under its sway.

[23] [Marx:] Templates [*Schablone*] is what one calls those stenciled forms over which house painters splash paint in order to throw borders, rosettes, etc. onto the walls, all fixed and uniform – in the manner of salon composers.

[24] Marx apparently invokes the idea of 2/4 meter here to show how this example, when so transformed, would indeed have an intermediate cadence at bar 4 – like any antecedent phrase.

broadly conceived *Satz*-like *Gang*, which, along with all that follows, needs no further discussion here. One will notice that this subsidiary *Satz* bears the same modulatory relation to its main *Satz* as that of the G major Sonata (p. 136),[25] but does not similarly turn to its minor mode; due to the greater power and vigor of the whole, it instead turns back toward its subdominant C major (with allusions to C minor in the closing *Satz*).

The subsidiary group as *Satz*-chain

On p. 139 we observed how a subsidiary group was curtailed out of consideration for the main group. In the following cases we shall find subsidiary groups that are expanded out of the same consideration, and indeed either simply to maintain a certain balance or equity between the groups, which one ought not readily disturb unless one has special grounds, or in order to complete something that may have been left undone in the main group.

We will intially observe the first of these concerns (which, as mentioned above, has nothing to do with an anxious counting of bars) in Beethoven's E♭ major Sonata, Op. 7. After an introductory onset, the main *Satz* enters at letter b (it is repeated on the dominant at c and then again on the tonic, an octave over b):

Example 4.62

---

[25] This is not strictly true; the G major Sonata modulated from G to B, whereas the *Hammerklavier* moves from B♭ to G (to the major submediant rather than the major mediant). On the other hand, both move to altered mediants which could be said to substitute for their unaltered versions. The *Hammerklavier* modulation is perhaps more radical, for it alters the relative minor of the home key, and uses this as its substitute dominant, while the G major work alters the relative minor of the dominant, and uses that as its substitute dominant.

A rather free inversion leads in the manner of a *Gang* back to the introductory motive a, which becomes a new little *Satz* [*Sätzchen*]:

Example 4.63

This carries on, over F to B♭ and the subsidiary *Satz*. This latter is similar to the main *Satz*, at least in its running eighth-note motion and in the use of free inversion upon its repetition. The two ideas formed from motive a in the main group thus lack a calming counterweight, and there can be no thought yet {281} of a closing *Satz* (which could be calming), since both main ideas have an almost *Gang*-like effect on account of their uniformly running eighth notes, and the whole still lacks the necessary stability [*Haltung*]. For this reason, a second *Satz* (a) appears, quietly rambling along in two beats per bar; sure enough, it too must again take up the running eighth notes, at the very end of its course and then during its repetition (b).

Example 4.64[26]

Yet as necessary as this richly felt idea clearly was, the need now arises again for the fiery animation of the beginning and then some. Thus a third, *Gang*-like, *Satz* must be introduced in affectingly urgent eighths and sixteenths and repeated with even stormier intensity. This brings on not a *Gang* (three of the five *Sätze* are already *Gang*-like) but a pedal point harmonically figured in sixteenth notes. —With this, the subsidiary group (eighty-seven bars at this point) has clearly exceeded the main group (forty bars) in extent and substance, displacing it from our minds. Consequently the closing *Satz* returns to a clearly stamped motive from the main group (the second one in Example 4.63), in order to shore up

---

[26] [Marx:] To be read an octave lower.

the main group even during the course of the now ascendant subsidiary group.

There is a similar state of affairs with the subsidiary group of the sonata from Example 4.21 [Op. 10, No. 3, in D]. After its first *Satz*, the main group introduces a second *Satz* in a different key and with different content (Example 4.23). The subsidiary group presents its first idea in the dominant (A major) and repeats it, as if with growing uncertainty, in A minor, pausing without resolution on a diminished seventh chord. Now a second *Satz* must follow; it alludes to the motive of the initial main *Satz*, first gently (a), then later more decisively (b):

Example 4.65

This leads to the closing *Satz*, which invokes the same motive: {282}

Example 4.66

This then brings on a second closing *Satz* in relaxed half notes. Now a *Satz* forms once again from the same motive, leading back to the beginning and into the Second Part.

In the C major Sonata, Op. 2, the first *Satz* (Example 4.9) is so sensible and proclaims the tonality so firmly, the second *Satz*, fashioned as a *Gang* (Example 4.43), is again so heartily firm about the main key, and the conclusion of the whole group is likewise formed so sharply and firmly on the dominant of the main key, that were the subsidiary *Satz* to act in accordance with the general law and appear immediately on the same dominant and in major, the whole would take on a quality of brilliant cheer that would border on frivolity – which would be due primarily to the particular content of the main group, namely to its daringly tossed off second *Satz*. But such a turn did not appeal to the composer; he prefers to bring his subsidiary *Satz* on in (!) G minor (instead of G major), and he repeats it in (!) D minor. As sensible as this change of course appears as a counterpoise to the bluffly styled main group, it strays far off the path in respect of its modulation. Consequently that first subsidiary *Satz*, as if it were not the right one, must turn from its G and D minor toward A minor (relative minor of the main key) and then lead a brief *Satz*-chain over G minor to a firm cadence in D major. Only now does a new, second *Satz* appear, relaxed and secure in G major – as if it alone were the right one. And yet, with all this the main group has receded into the distance. —Hence that hearty motive (Example 4.43) reappears, as boldly as before, in the form of a *Gang*; after a closing *Satz* that breaks off in the manner of the very first idea of the movement (Example 4.9), it asserts itself again as the final closing gesture.

In this example it is first a matter of avoiding an effect of onesidedness that would arise by taking the direct path from the main group to a normatively placed subsidiary group, and next of getting back on course after this evasive deviation. As mentioned above, the sonata presented in Example 4.11a [Op. 10, No. 2, in F] contains no modulation at all to the dominant (much less through the dominant of the dominant, from F over G to C); instead, there is a succinct cadence on the dominant of A minor, at which point the subsidiary *Satz* enters: {283}

Example 4.67

Not only does this arrive without the usual preparation of an emphatic modulation, but it also bears an unmistakable resemblance to the initial main idea and is subsequently – despite its charm – inadequate as a second main idea. This circumstance impels the composer onward; the *Satz* becomes a *Gang* leading to G major, this key (dominant of the dominant) is then imprinted most emphatically, and now a second *Satz* follows (in C major, then C minor, since C major has already doubled its effect), with subsequent *Gang* and closing *Satz*.— In a similar sense, Mozart's C minor Sonata (Example 4.35) brings on the dominant of the subsidiary group (B♭ in the key of E♭) only after the first *Satz* of that group, and then lets a second *Satz* follow. In both cases, a swifter and more vigorous progression is attained, and the law of modulation is still propitiated.

SECTION FOUR: THE SECOND AND THIRD PARTS

After the discussion that has already taken place, namely in the fourth through eighth sections of Part Four, we can now get by with less comprehensive and exhaustive instances; both the essential events – what is the purpose and the content of the Second and Third Parts? – as well as the applied laws governing the formation of *Satz* and period, and the opening up of these into *Gänge*, etc., are already familiar to us and have been sufficiently illustrated in examples.

The Second Part

In the sonata form, as in all forms, this part is *the motion-oriented part*. Even the *Sätze* and the periods that appear within it belong to the element of motion. This is already apparent in the following ways: they no longer appear in the main key or the most closely related key; they appear in altered forms and are thus led away from their original essence; they are opened up into *Gänge* or terminated and led into other *Sätze*; or they are not even required to appear at all in the Second Part, but instead may be alternately preferred – now the main *Satz*, now the subsidiary *Satz*, and, with the presence of more *Sätze* in {284} the main or subsidiary groups, now this *Satz* or now that – or simply passed over. Now, in concept, however, the essence of motion is limitless, as opposed to the sharply determined essence of the *Satz*, or moment of repose. *The Satz* must limit itself, it must set an end for itself – and indeed a specific and necessary end. *The Gang* has in and of itself no necessary end at all; it is broken off, because it simply cannot go on forever and because the higher concerns of the whole call the composer away to other configurations. Thus the *Satz* has a specific place in the key scheme; it belongs wholly or primarily to one key center and must obey certain laws of harmonic progression, without which there can be no closure. The *Gang*, on the other hand, has no specific place in the key scheme; it can just as easily go through whatever keys it pleases as remain in one key, and it can take up or reject any motive, again as it pleases.

This freedom in the choice of material, in its ordering, in modulation, and in extent, is peculiar to the Second Part of sonata form.

Content of the Second Part

If *the main Satz* is of preponderant interest, then it becomes the exclusive, or predominant, concern of the Second Part. This is the case in Beethoven's *Pathétique* Sonata, where, after an intermediary *Satz* taken from the introduction (and which is totally foreign to the actual existence of the main block of material), the main *Satz* appears – or, at the least, a *Satz* fashioned after it (compare a of Example 4.68 with Example 4.5):

Example 4.68

It is heard twice in the upper voice, then (in accord with the primary matter, a) three times in the bass – in E minor, G/D, F, B♭, and C minor – and then reaches the pedal point through a brief *Gang*-like continuation. So, too, in the E minor Sonata, Op. 90, where the main *Satz* was already the predominant concern of the First Part; in the Second Part, first its main motive (a in Example 4.14), and then its second motive (section e of Example 4.14), are led through separately. Both motives are inwardly immersed in the same sense that inspirits the whole. {285} The same goes for the sonata observed in Example 4.2, in which both *Sätze* of the main group (Examples 4.2 and 4.4) come into account.

In other cases it is *the subsidiary Satz* that is granted admission to the Second Part. We see this most decisively in the great E♭ major Sonata of Haydn, where, after a fleeting memory from the close of the First Part, the subsidiary *Satz* enters in E major, is broadly carried out in the manner of a *Gang*, and reappears in C major.

Cases in which main and subsidiary *Satz* are used together appear more frequently. It must even be confessed that this is what happens, at bottom, in the composition just mentioned. The subsidiary *Satz* indeed predominates indisputably as the main affair, yet part of the main *Satz* finds an opportunity, within the *Gang*, to make itself heard. Conversely, in the C♯ minor Sonata (Example 4.13) the motive of the main *Satz* serves as an introduction, taking us from the dominant to the subdominant. At this point, the subsidiary *Satz* is played in its entirety in the upper voice, then in the lower voice, with a cadence that moves to G major, and is then repeated with a turn toward C♯ minor whereupon it is led, with a *Gang*-like application of its final motive, to the pedal point.

We see the same thing in the F minor Sonata, observed in Example 4.11. The First Part had closed in A♭ major; the Second Part begins with the first section of the main *Satz* (Example 4.11, a) in that same key, positions itself on the dominant with the repetition of the last bar, then repeats section a and moves, again with the repetition of the last bar, to the dominant of B♭ minor, the subdominant of the main key. At this point the subsidiary *Satz* enters for eight bars, with a turn toward C minor (dominant of the main key), is heard there for two times two bars (repeating Example 4.55) in the upper voice, then two more bars in the bass, is moved, again in the bass, to the dominant of B♭ minor and back again to that of A♭ minor (the minor mode of the relative major – reached here by a stepwise descent from C minor through B♭ minor to A♭ minor), and is now led, thoroughly in the manner of a *Gang*, to the pedal point, where a motive from the main *Satz* (b in Example 4.12) ultimately invites a return to the same, and to the Third Part.

Beethoven takes the same path in the great F minor Sonata (p. 111). The First Part closed in A♭ minor; after turning from that key to E major (a♭–c♭–e♭, g♯–b–d♯, g♯–b–e), the Second Part opens with the head of the main *Satz*:

Example 4.69

{286} This forms the basis of a *Satz*-chain, in which the *Satz* is sounded, alternating every two bars, in the upper and lower voices (the first notes fall away in the upper voice, as they find no space there next to the equally significant countermelody [*Gegenstimme*]), and taking this course to the dominant of D♭ major:[27]

Example 4.70

---

[27] [Marx:] At first glance, Beethoven conceals the last harmony referred to in Example 4.70, substituting an a for a b♭♭ (for ease of reading). He also alternates between the chords a♭–c–e♭–g♭ and c–e♭–g♭–b♭♭; as this is inessential, it is not given in the example.

On this dominant, in the manner of a pedal point, the introduction to the subsidiary *Satz* from the First Part appears – only now further developed – and, after it, the tonic D♭ of the subsidiary *Satz* itself. This then turns to B♭ minor at its cadence, repeats itself in full, and turns further, to G♭ major, where another presentation of its first section is heard that includes the final motive (b):

Example 4.71

Only now will this lead, through free arpeggiations, to the pedal point from which the Third Part immediately enters with the main *Satz*.

The same thing can again be seen in Mozart's C minor Sonata (Example 4.35). Even within the First Part, the antecedent phrase of the main *Satz* is introduced in E♭ major after the closing *Satz* and closed with a turn toward C minor. It thus serves first to lead back to the beginning (and the repetition of the First Part) and then as a bridge into the Second Part. This moves to the subdominant, using the main motive (a) and the counter *Satz* already familiar from Example 4.38:

Example 4.72

{287} Then the first *Satz* of the subsidiary group (four bars) enters, followed by the main motive in F minor, then on the dominant and tonic of G minor, then on the dominant, tonic, and dominant again of C minor. After a brief (five-bar) pedal point, the Third Part commences.

At times it is the *closing Satz*, and not the subsidiary *Satz*, that vies with the main *Satz* for the commanding interest. A very straightforward instance of this is found in Beethoven's D major Sonata Op. 28, in which the (first) subsidiary *Satz* has formed itself completely in accordance with the sense of the whole, but not in such a way that its influence could be brought to bear in the Second Part, along with, or in place of, the main *Satz*. There the noble minded main *Satz* (indeed the initial one, from Example 4.17) enters first again, in the subdominant G major, and is repeated with attractive variation in G minor. Now it has captivated our interest and will not soon let it go. Its last bars are heard on the dominant, with a new counter *Satz*:

Example 4.73

Then the voices switch (as if a small fugato were in the making), sound again over tonic and dominant, and build a further *Gang* and pedal point on the dominant of B, primarily with the motive from the last bar; this quietly arrives at a conclusion. With this the main *Satz* has been so sufficiently aired that it could neither be pursued further nor brought back immediately by commencing the Third Part. The quiescent subsidiary *Satz* is also of no help here; consequently the charming closing *Satz* appears in its stead, first in B major and then in B minor – and with the repetition of its last phrase, the music moves to the main key and into the Third Part.

The Eb Sonata [Op. 7] mixes ideas from main *Satz* and closing *Satz* even more rapidly. After the first idea of the main *Satz* (Example 4.62, a) and a free two-voice passage in eighth notes, a rather long-range play with a motive from the closing *Satz* takes place, followed by a return to the first motive of the main *Satz*, heard twice (with a new continuation).

In the C major Sonata [Op. 53] (Example 4.15), the last section of the closing *Satz* serves to lead into the subdominant (from E minor and C major). The main *Satz* enters here and guides the music, with the aid of a *Gang*-like motive that was appended to the subsidiary *Satz* in the First Part, to the pedal point and the Third Part.

Finally, in the Second Part of the great Bb major Sonata [Op. 106] {288} we see the most comprehensive use of the main group and of the close – we must use this expression here [i.e. close instead of closing *Satz*], because this most comprehensive of all piano works presents two closing *Sätze* along with the many *Sätze* of the main and subsidiary groups: one for the purpose of attaining some calm after the highly intensified subsidiary *Satz*, the other for a bolder close and for a way back to the beginning and into the Second Part. The final closing *Satz* (G major), which had even managed to bring on an allusion to the first motive of the whole, now leads us, at the beginning of the Second Part, to the keys of C minor and E♭ major. Here that first motive (the first four notes of Example 4.49) is the subject of a broadly conceived imitative *Satz*:

Example 4.74

This two-voice *Satz* builds to three and four voices, leads to the first closing *Satz* in B major, and then arises again in that key, in order to move to B♭ major and then proceed immediately to the main group of the Third Part.

Modulation

Just as varied as the deployment of content in the Second Part is that of modulation. Of course the fundamental precepts of modulation still apply in general. Thus one does not let the keys of the First and Third Parts – the tonic, the dominant (in major), or the relative major (in minor) – come to the fore within the Second Part, or (these latter keys) only in cases in which they have not been used in the First Part. Furthermore, one will tend toward the most closely related and most requisite keys rather than more distant keys. And yet, in the motion-oriented Second Part more than anywhere else, numerous – and the most freely conceived – deviations from this are both possible and appropriate, as long as they have their foundation in the progress [*Gang*] and content of the whole. No further examples of this are required here; enough have already been given in the preceding discussion. Nor can we permit ourselves to enter once more into the question of motivation for more remote modulations; about this just as much enlightenment has been vouchsafed in the foregoing as a doctrine of form can possibly offer without profoundly exploring the particular content of art works.

The Third Part

The chief task of the Third Part is to repeat the First Part, but of course in such a way that the subsidiary group is put into the main key as well. Yet in addition, we must never lose sight of the fact that it is very closely allied with the {289} Second and First Parts and thus must always take into consideration their course of progress, supplying, when necessary, anything that was omitted in those earlier Parts. This can be managed, however, in the greatest variety of ways, of which we offer only a few examples to stimulate further study on the part of the student.

1 In the F major Sonata (Example 4.11a, Op. 10, No. 2), the first and most attractive idea of the subsidiary group appeared without sufficient modulatory preparation (p. 145) and was so closely related to the main *Satz* that one would be tempted to count it as part of the main group if its key center did not contradict this. The Third Part takes advantage of this; it attaches the equivocal *Satz* directly to the main *Satz*, such that both together constitute a block of material not joined by a mediating link but rather formed as an unmediated amalgamation, as if it were a single idea. Only with this subsidiary *Satz* does the music go to the dominant and then proceed regularly from there.

2 The C minor *Pathétique* Sonata establishes its subsidiary *Satz* (Example 4.60) in E♭ minor rather than E♭ major, arriving only later at E♭ major; in the Second Part, the main harmonic event even appears to be E minor, because that is where the main *Satz* is heard. The Third Part goes from the main *Satz* in C minor to the subdominant F minor, in order to bring on the subsidiary *Satz* in this key; only upon repetition is the subsidiary *Satz* heard in C minor. Through this process the subsidiary *Satz* is profiled just as sharply as in the First Part, with its use of E♭ minor – but here the main key is increasingly reinforced … at the same time. Nevertheless, the introduction and main *Satz* ultimately return one more time, naturally in the main key, as a coda – and, indeed, not without regard to what has already gone on.

3 The main idea of the C♯ minor Sonata (Example 4.13), despite all the energy of its content (or, rather, for the sake of it), is predicated simply enough upon the one motive of its antecedent *Satz*, and the opening of its consequent *Satz* is practically a mere repetition of the first *Satz*.

The Third Part completely discards this consequent *Satz* and goes directly from the broad cadence of the antecedent *Satz* to the subsidiary *Satz*, in the manner of a sonatina. Now, however, after a complete presentation of the subsidiary *Satz* and closing *Satz*, the motive of the main *Satz* is again heard, in the subdominant, as part of a coda, whereupon the main idea of the subsidiary group is repeated in the main key, first with a new continuation and finally with the old closing *Satz*. It is the same formation as in 1 above, only for a different reason.[28]

4 In the great C major Sonata (Example 4.15, Op. 53) the subsidiary *Satz*, as we know, appeared in E major, and the First Part came to a close in E minor. Without exploring the deeper foundation of this move, one must immediately acknowledge it as striking; it entices merely by dint of its {290} foreign quality. Thus it must not be allowed to go missing in the Third Part; were the subsidiary *Satz* to appear immediately in C major, as is normal, it would clearly be the loser over and against the First Part. — Now, that E major in the First Part (p. 118) was actually substituted for E minor, which was itself substituted for G major. In the same way, the subsidiary *Satz* appears in the Third Part in A major (instead of A minor instead of C major); it does not remain there, however (as did the First Part in E major), but is immediately repeated in A minor with a turn to C major and then twice repeated in C. Thus it takes the same course in actuality that we attributed to the composer in thought.[29] The rest follows normally; but since the pensively quiet closing *Satz* cannot provide a satisfying close for the splendid and fiery animation of the whole, it is jolted to Db major (just as the beginning of the sonata went from C to Bb and from C to D), where the main *Satz* is heard. After a far-ranging realization, the subsidiary *Satz* and then finally the main *Satz* are both heard, back in the main key. This comprehensive coda befits the richness of a boldly modeled movement.

[28] Marx refers here to the main body of the recapitulation, not to the coda he has just finished describing. Like that of 1, this recapitulation proceeds directly from the main *Satz* to the subsidiary *Satz*.

[29] [Marx:] Let us once again repel the misunderstanding that would assume that the composer thought out his course in complete logical detail. He was probably attracted so powerfully only by the splendor and general sense of his subsidiary key (E major). But our intellectual examination proves that this is not an aberration, not just some seductive delusion.

5 We see the same thing in the G major Sonata [Op. 31, No. 1]. Its
   subsidiary *Satz* appeared in B major and B minor in the First Part
   (Example 4.56); in the Third Part it thus appears in E major and E
   minor but is then presented two more times in G major. With this,
   however, the main *Satz* has been supplanted in a worrisome fashion,
   all the more so because it has not been repeated at the beginning, as
   in the First Part. Consequently, a coda first brings back the relevant
   Gang (Example 4.32) with the broad half cadence, following this
   with a charmingly tender close, which is fashioned from the main
   motive itself:

Example 4.75

Here the mischievous doings of the main *Satz* are ultimately suffused
with a more inwardly touching emotion, as this most attractive of
metamorphoses yet remains true to the fundamental note of the
piece's mood {291} – just as in the midst of some rambunctious
child's play one detects, with surprise, the hint of a thoughtful reverie
more suited to a maidenly age, only to see it disappear soon again in
the sparkling joy of childhood.

6 The far-reaching Bb major Sonata [Op. 106] (Example 4.49) pursues
   its bold modulations in the Third Part as well. The first main *Satz*
   appears in the main key, the second in Gb major, then again in B
   minor (subdominant of F#/Gb). From here there is a modulation
   back to the main key; only now does the complete subsidiary group,
   supported by a broad coda powerfully formed from the main motive
   of the first idea, sufficiently round off the harmonic trajectory and
   establish a sense of repose.

PART III

HERMENEUTIC ANALYSIS AND THE *IDEE*

LUDWIG VAN BEETHOVEN: LIFE AND WORKS
SELECTED EXCERPTS

Ludwig van Beethoven: Leben und Schaffen, 3rd edn, ed. Dr. Gustav Behncke (Berlin:Verlag von Otto Janke, 1875),Vol. I

The following excerpts, from Marx's life-and-works biography of Beethoven, first published in 1859, demonstrate above all the central importance of the "Eroica" Symphony within Marx's musical thought. It was this work that enjoined Marx to declare a new era in music, one that "cannot be superseded."

Marx devotes three chapters to the "Eroica" in his Beethoven biography. The first of these, "The consecration of the hero," presents Marx's programmatic analysis of the "Eroica." The overriding point of Marx's analysis is to show how Beethoven's music is capable of embodying an Idea. For Marx, the first movement represents an Ideal image of Napoleon's heroic life, summed up in Marx's terse formulation: "Napoleon was battle." The ensuing dramatic program thus charts the course of an idealized battle, from the morning on the battlefield to the celebration of victory. Marx's analysis manifests the usual bias toward first movements; in this case, his analysis of the first movement is at least three times longer than that of the rest of the movements combined.

In the second chapter, "The "Eroica" Symphony and ideal music," Marx outlines three stages of music history, in order to place Beethoven and his "Eroica" Symphony at the culmination of that history. Marx's triadic view of music history tracks the evolving role of musical art in human affairs: the first stage is that of the blessed play [*Spielseligkeit*] of tones, the second that of the representation of feelings, the third that of ideal music. In this latter stage, music is able to portray objective scenarios of the highest human import and drama. Each stage continues to be preserved within those that follow, in the manner of a Hegelian historical process.

Finally, Marx's third chapter, "The future before the tribunal of the past," defends some of the symphony's bolder passages against the judgements of other critics.

THE CONSECRATION OF THE HERO

{245} Let us now turn to the work itself.

What did Beethoven want? What could he give? Some composition or other of great size and magnificence? That is what our aestheticians would have advised him to do, namely those, both old and new, who attribute to music nothing but a play of forms, or who figure that it aims at only the most general arousal of vague moods, because it is incapable of "expressing that which is concrete." Beethoven was of another mind. As an artist he had nothing to do with lifeless abstractions; like all artists, his vocation was to create life out of his own life. The artist, alone and above all, knows of what his art is capable. But this is the failing of almost all philosophers of art, that they neglect the testimony of artists and artworks, in order to spin the threads of their abstraction without being disconcerted.[1]

Even such a thing as a new "military" symphony in the manner of Haydn's, with trumpet flourishes and bass drum, would have been unseemly in this case.

{246} Beethoven seized his task in the only way worthy of itself and its object, the only artistic way. Not a trace of those abstractions that leave our art nothing beyond the idea that something – one knows not what – is formed, and something – one knows not what – is felt or sensed. This would be an art for playful maidens, incapable of, and unfit for, anything further, and not for men like Beethoven, Bach, and all free artists. —And, naturally, there is no trace of that historical concretion [*Konkretismus*] that provides names, dates, and the complete content of the events and souls involved. Of this, music is not capable, but, then again, it does not want to be, because it is art.

For Beethoven, Napoleon was *the hero*, who, like any other of these world-shaking heroes – whether named Alexander, or Dionysus, or Napoleon – embraces the world with his Idea and his will and marches across it, as a victor at the head of an army of heroes, in order to fashion it anew. This was no genre-idea [*Genre-Gedanke*], no portrait of Napoleon the man and his battles; what grew within Beethoven was an ideal image in the genuine Greek sense. Moreover, it was not even an iconic image of the hero but rather a complete drama of the Napoleonic life; it

---

[1] [Marx:] The author has already discussed the decisive question in an earlier work, *Über Malerei in der Tonkunst, ein Maigruss an die Kunstphilosophen*, 1828.

found its germinal seed in the campaigns against the north and south, east and west, in the "*hundred victorious battles*," to use Napoleon's own designation. And since the poet's job is not to grasp the *breadth* of life but rather the *acme*, the *Idea*, of it, the *battle* was thus the necessary first event in Beethoven's program [*Aufgabe*]. *The battle* – not this or that specific battle (as Beethoven later wrote the battle of Vittoria and others, e.g. *Jadin*, wrote the battles of Austerlitz and Jena) but the battle as *ideal image*.[2] And this {247} only in the sense that the battle is the decisive moment, the acme, of the hero's life.

In this sense, and in accordance with inner necessity, the first act of the symphony, the ideal battle, initiates the spiritual image of the heroic process [*Heldengang*], which emerges from a quiet, barely noticeable, beginning and soon traverses the world.

Allegro con brio

Example 5.1

After two powerful blows of the entire orchestra ("Hark! Hark!"), the heroic idea [*Heldengedanke*] – marked in Example 5.1 with A – appears

---

[2] [Marx:] This is no arbitrary assertion, much less a pretentious art-philosophical phrase, but an actual, demonstrable truth; and it appears of great importance for the secure interpretation of the heroic symphony that this point is confirmed.

If Beethoven's intentions ran only to a depiction of battle, then there would be no content left for the next three movements, no place left for them in the rest of the art work; the first movement alone offers the depiction of battle – if such a depiction was intended in some sense – and with this movement the artwork would be concluded. Thus the existence of the three following movements already proves that the task of the tone poet was not simply a depiction of battle.

If it were Beethoven's intention to represent a specific battle – no matter how one might judge such a task and the means to its solution – then this battle would have to be specifically designated. This is what Beethoven did later with the battle of Vittoria. Regimental music (in addition to the full orchestra) designates the armies, well-known folk tunes tell us that France and England are the adversaries, while the thunder of cannons and firing of artillery, the charges, etc. complete the concrete image, marking it as a generic one [*bis in das Genrehafte*]. The battles of Austerlitz and Jena and countless other constructions of this sort are also painted in similar manner, with national marches, cavalry fanfares, and all the rubbish of real battles – and this goes for all other representations of this sort.

Of all this there is no trace here; nothing whatever happens for the sake of a concrete image of a battle, everything here is ideal, even the passages characteristic of battle are not there for the sake of the battle, for the sake of their own deployment, but are only features which complete the image of Napoleon's character. *Napoleon was battle.*

quietly in the violoncellos under the cover of pulsing eighth notes in the second violins and violas, only to dissipate again with the sharp breeze that drifts toward G minor. Yet events turn immediately back to the main key (E♭ major), and the heroic idea sets in again, this time in flute, clarinet, and horn, spanning three octaves, in order to allow the main *Satz* to take hold more firmly. There is something extremely suspenseful lurking in this preparation. The main idea appears in the violoncellos as a still faint presence emanating but little heat – like the sun when it just touches the horizon – and then, again like the sun, hides itself once more in chilling mists. This sense of "not yet!" (how often this has been pronounced by Napoleon in the heat of battle, when his generals call for the reserves too soon!), this dissipation into the relative minor of the dominant extends the *Satz* from four bars to thirteen bars: this puts us in mind of affairs of great moment.[3]

Now the main idea, the sun over the battlefield, has returned in octaves in the winds, higher, warmer, and ruling (it was at first a lower voice) – {248} yet still gentle and friendly, like field music on the morning of the battle. Violins and basses lead it toward a gloomier F minor, and again flutes, clarinets, and bassoon appear at the fore; but it is the violins, already supported by the full orchestra – only trumpets and drums are still lacking – that lead the *Satz* to its completion on the dominant.

Example 5.2

Though they are yet to play their real roles, those vaulting passages at B and the sharply piercing syncopes at C already announce themselves;

---

[3] This description is remarkably similar to Oulibicheff's account of the opening – so close, in fact, that Marx must be borrowing from it. See Aléxandre Oulibicheff, *Beethoven, ses critiques, ses glossateurs* (Leipzig: F. A. Brockhaus, 1857), 175. For a superb account of this and other intertextual traces in Marx's interpretation, see Thomas Sipe, "Interpreting Beethoven: History, Aesthetics, and Critical Reception" (Ph.D. diss., University of Pennsylvania, 1992), pp. 296–304.

here their intensity rises only to a cheerfully defiant resolve. And finally the hero's word now sounds, powerfully broadcast and turned toward darker resolve in the combined voices of the basses, violas, bassoons, clarinets, oboes and flutes, horns and – only now! – trumpets, all under the buzzing violins and confirming roar of the tympani.

Example 5.3[4]

This is the hero on his throne, the battle steed.

A peculiarly characteristic idea (subsidiary *Satz* on the dominant, B♭ major) now joins in (see D in Example 5.4): {249}

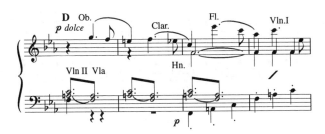

Example 5.4

This draws quietly nearer, like joyfully exulting field music sounding from a distance. Though internally whole, externally it seems disconnected into fragmented limbs, emerging now in this instrument and now in that – first in the oboe, then in the clarinet, then in the flute, then in the first violin, and again through them all: as if one surveyed the vast battlefield from a hilltop, blinking into the radiance of the morning sun that flashes in and among the shining weapons, and hearing from afar the bright call of field music preceding the troops massing here and there. Now everything masses more tightly together, everyone steps more cheerfully, sure footed amid the flash and clash of their weapons (E in Example 5.5), and they all join together, man to man, troop to troop, the whole inspired with high courage, like one body with one mighty will.

---

[4] [Marx:] The examples, let it be said once and for all, give only intimations; whoever desires the complete view must turn to the score – or assist himself with piano editions.

Example 5.5

That this is humanly conceived, and that it is the truly artistic opposite of all the swaggering clatter of real arms, is revealed by the reflective imaginings (F, in Example 5.6) that now, in the face of bloody resolution, steal upon the soul and threaten to grow yet gloomier. {250}

Example 5.6

At this point everyone draws together under the encouraging word of the hero (G in Example 5.7) – at first uncertainly, then ever more briskly and concertedly, as with flags flying.

Example 5.7

Now all rush forth to the fray, breasts heaving amid the bustle of their fellow warriors, forth to those hard blows that shred the prevailing rhythm, forth to the decision, which, with a furious shriek of the entire orchestra, returns the hero's call and wills its affirmation.

Example 5.8

Thus the First Part.[5] It has conjured up for us the image of battle. This was what Beethoven had to offer, this and nothing other. But battle is war; it is the career of the hero, the complete hero, this Briareus with a hundred thousand arms for whom the world was too narrow.[6] Such a vision hovers before the tone poet, only he compresses and concentrates what is general into a single, energetic course of events, in the manner of all {251} art, just as the *Iliad* compressed a ten-year war into the span of a few days.[7] We will need to maintain this perspective through the rest of the movement's progress as well.

The hero's call has been answered emphatically. But it sinks into shadows; an anxious moment holds everything suspended (the first fifteen bars of the Second Part), as a foothold is sought only hesitantly amid vacillations and helplessness.—

Worthy of admiration is the way Beethoven gets rhythm to obey him, or rather, the way his will – for the determining will embodies itself in rhythm – remains the faithful servant of his Idea. The main *Satz* (A) enters with secure, evenly weighted steps, which become enlivened.

Example 5.9

The firm command (E) makes a domineering appearance in short fragments: a word suffices.

[5] I.e., what we would call the exposition.

[6] In Greek mythology, Briareus is a hundred-handed giant. Marx appears to be multiplying for the sake of hyperbole – his hero is a Briareus who now has a hundred *thousand* arms. This, after all, is not a bad image for a modern-day general.

[7] Carolyn Abbate cites this passage as evidence of an epic mode in Marx's view of musical narration, "in which a narrating voice retells or recounts events retrospectively, and at a critical distance." Abbate, *Unsung Voices: Opera and Musical Narrative in the Nineteenth Century* (Princeton: Princeton University Press, 1991), 23.

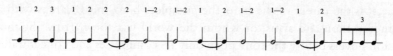

Example 5.10

Those belligerent syncopes that first showed up at C, only slightly developed, and were immediately thereafter further confirmed (in one of the
transitional passages – who could hope to relate all of this?), tear wildly
at the prevailing order, so as to fly back to the main *Satz*, which establishes a sense of security.

Example 5.11

In that moment of hesitation [i.e. at the beginning of the Second Part],
syncopes indeed form again after the unmistakable stagnation of the A
rhythm, but they are such as can only paralyze.

Example 5.12

One need only perceive these rhythms tonelessly, as with drumbeats, to
become aware of their pure significance. But these are just isolated instances; the rhythm in its entirety is spirit.—

   Everything has come to a halt. The field music (D) sounds again,
{252} as from afar, calling out in friendly encouragement (dolce!—)
with a more vigorous onset (H); it leads back to the *matter at hand*.

Example 5.13

The basses then sound the call, in a coldly dark C minor.

Example 5.14

The violins intensify the call and urge it toward the harsh key of D minor, while over its commanding word the heated conflict erupts and the full choir of winds (excepting trumpets and drums) spreads out in victoriously confident rhythms.[8]

Example 5.15

This battle scene has spread itself broadly, taking its first stand in D minor (in the last example, which is missing four bars on {253} a–c♯–e–g) and its second (another eight bars) in G minor. Now the field music (D) drifts over a great distance from A major [sic: Marx means A♭ major]; a severe struggle, as in hand-to-hand combat, breaks out around it, motivated by it. Here are a few bars from the middle of this – only those that are easiest to illustrate:

[8] But trumpets are included here.

Example 5.16

Hard blows now pierce through in the sharp bow strokes of the strings, without any ameliorating winds; they rise up with urgent passion, again in the syncopes heard above at C and heard now amid the cries of the entire orchestra.

Example 5.17

This struggle, too, is greatly extended (thirty-three bars, counting the previous *Satz*), passing in broad waves over A minor, E minor, and B minor toward C major; it finally comes to a stand on an evil chord, choir against unshakable choir (all the winds against all the strings, with a third horn adding its own shout), like two men fighting chest to chest; and then breaks off suddenly, dying out with hard pulses on b–d♯–f♯–a–c and b–d♯–f♯–a to end in E minor.

Let us interrupt ourselves once again.

Up to now this musical poem [*Tongedicht*] has stayed strictly within the lines of sonata form, only with dimensions that leave all previous works behind and not to be compared. This expansion was necessary for content that before would have been unthinkably rich for a single movement. Greater space was needed, and that means enlarged modulation. That this great expansion and far extended circle of modulation results in neither debility nor confusion, nor even any uncertainty, stands as witness to the precision of Beethoven's vision and to his formative energy. Each *Satz* is rounded off in a fully plastic fashion and solidly established; indeed, the upward growth of each happens before our eyes and we begin to live along with its {254} life, such that we never forget it. Another *Satz* appears after it, and we are fully prepared to take it up. This is a triumph of spirit as well as form – if one were to hazard a division of that which is inseparably one. We hold it no virtue on the part of Beethoven to cling to previous forms, since he surely both possessed and exercised the power and the right to supersede the forms handed down by his predecessors, or to deviate from them entirely. We want only to have pointed out that the given form was satisfactory for his completely new content and for the expansion of the entire structure.

But now he deviates from this form – or at least from all previous manifestations of it. He has to do so, for a wholly new idea demands to be heard.

Immediately following the cadence on E [minor] this idea is expressed by idiosyncratically selected voices:

Example 5.18

Is this sorrow over the sacrifice; is it a prophetic warning, not yet understood; is it some voice of distant memory, perhaps from that place where "forty centuries" saw heroes, victories, and retreats? Strange the sound of this song, raised aloft by the delicately aware oboes, taken up by the sharply lamenting violoncellos, which are indeed augmented by the second violins and yet made milder; strange, too, the way the flutes mix their monotone, flat and hollow sounding b with the rhythmic surges of the first violins; strange, how the bass confirms all of this with quiet, tympani-like strokes. The consequent phrase turns to A minor, where flutes and bassoons repeat the song over floating strings.

What is this?— It is one of the riddles of the human heart, {255} one of those riddling voices that sometimes sound their way into the destiny of men, just like the whispered words that Brutus heard on the lips of dying Caesar. Such secrets escape the "common intelligibility of things."

All this holds no claim on the hero's life. The hero's word, the leader's will, enters with coldly decisive strides in the bright key of C major, carried in massive concord by all the strings, bassoons, and swelling oboes. Extended with prodigious force – this is not unprepared, as B (in Example 5.2) shows – amidst the acclamation of trumpets and driving thrusts in the horns, it rises over all the voices, to be repeated, more darkly now, in C minor.

Example 5.19

In vain the call of warning, or lament, sounds again with increased urgency; it is extinguished, and the hero's call sounds everywhere, along with the stormy stride of the basses (which appeared already at C in Example 5.2 and in Example 5.17).

Example 5.20[9]

The call echoes from troop to troop, in the bassoons, clarinets, oboes, and flutes, again in bassoons, horns, and clarinets, then again in oboes and flutes; it drives far afield and dies out quivering, as widely spaced horns[10] reverberate from a great distance like final sighs amid the gasps of the other winds; into this the strings and their pizzicati fall like distant cannonfire. {256}

---

[9] [Marx:] In this presentation, as in almost all the rest, most of the filler and accompanying tones are lacking.

[10] [Marx:] The horns lie a twelfth apart and are thus isolated from each other. The lower horn in this register has something coarse in its sound, the upper horn something effusive; thus they separate themselves from the accompanying bassoons and flutes, over which an oboe sounds. One takes to heart here the character of a fifth ... , which, as a twelfth (1:3), attains a more pronounced effect of forlorn uncertainty.

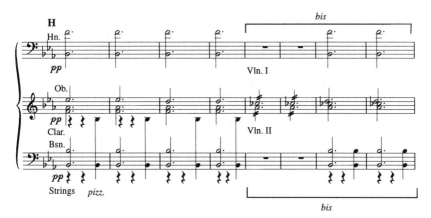

Example 5.21

And to these dying strains, from far, far away, drifts the sound of the call!

Example 5.22

It is not necessary to follow the plot any further as it continues into the Third Part and ends in the radiance of victory. The conclusion of the whole act does not merely proclaim the triumph of the hero, but also the triumph of the movement itself, whose decisive features are brought together into one event. It begins in bar [631] of the score, with the combination of the *Satz* we have often referred to as the hero's word and a *Satz* built from one of the figures in Example 5.5 (at E), which, as it descends, picks up the eighth-note figure from H (Example 5.13); for now we will designate these three elements as A, B, and C.

Example 5.23

{257} A appears initially in the first horn and B in the first violin, with C following. Then the second horn, which in the excitement of the moment seemed to enter prematurely (bar 4 in Example 5.23), in the company of the oboe, repeats the phrase, again with the first violin, now on the dominant – tonic and dominant alternate continuously in this way. Next, the second violin takes B, the first takes A, and the three horns lend a most graceful encouragement to A with their gently penetrating resonance, while clarinets and violas play an accompanying figure (as second violin did before by itself) and declaim, with oboes and flutes, the fifth that seems to look out at everything from on high.

Example 5.24

Now the basses take up A; flutes, clarinets, bassoons, and finally oboes as well join in with an ascending and descending C; horns and violins fill in (the latter with syncopations); and trumpets and drums, still *piano*, announce themselves with the following rhythmic swagger:

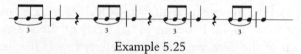

Example 5.25

Finally, the trumpets and all the winds call out and confirm the hero's word, amid the continuous thunder of the tympani, while the basses and bassoons unfurl the countertheme (B and C). The whole is an evolution in splendidly broad layers of four times eight bars. Never has victory been more brilliantly celebrated. The image of war is now complete, the idea of the first movement fully realized and spiritually exhausted. Any further working out would be repetition, with the same, or with different, notes.

Beethoven will not return to these things. It is his way to execute an idea completely and then to step forth resolutely to the next.—

The *second act*, Adagio assai, is labeled Marcia funebre {258} and indeed appears in that form. One knows from the Sonata Op. 26 how

Beethoven writes a "Funeral march on the death of a hero." Here in the symphony his task is completely different and more comprehensive; the superscript is only an indication, offering a first clue as to the interpretation. One is convinced of this just as soon as one hears beyond the first subsections of the movement and pulls together the entire context. At the same time, the artistic forms [*Kunstformen*] are so firmly grounded [in Beethoven] that the fundamental features of the March with Trio order the entire content.[11]

If the first act depicted the battle – as the epitome of the hero's life – now evening has arrived, and with it the onerous procession on the battleground, now so still. The choir of strings appears first, with basses playing muffled rolls; the choir of winds, accompanied by muffled tympani, follows in step amid the now shivering strings. With its precise intensity, the oboe leads the melody, while clarinets, bassoons, and horns accompany with uncomplicated demure; only the lament of the first horn stands out, its fifth, g1, placed oddly aloft (for this scoring!). The turn from the main key of C minor to its parallel, E♭ major, is brief and grand. Here the Second Part enters in the strings, very quietly and yet with composure. But these thoughts soon lose themselves again to gloomy brooding, and the deep, melancholy voice of the violoncello wanders in lonely aimlessness until the grave procession starts up again, graver still for entering in the subdominant. The winds lead a repetition of the entire Second Part, with a swelling orchestra that enlarges upon all the imaginings that awaken in such a somber hour. A further appendix [*Anhang*] closes this earnest scene with magnificent concentration.

Beethoven would not have possessed human feelings did he not now wake the soothing voice of consolation. The gentle C major song enters in oboes, then flute, then bassoon, over strings that are now drawing deep breaths of relief and stirring with fresh life – an alternating dialogue is already perceptible in their lower voices. There is no doubt but that the sweetness of dying for the fatherland and for freedom is being praised here,[12] for the entire army of the orchestra answers with the brightest cry of triumph, bringing on trumpet fanfares for the first time, along with thundering tympani. How these ideas reach even further (in the second part of the Trio, to speak in terms of form), such that high heaven itself seems to smile down upon the fallen hero, and are again

[11] On the meaning and significance of the term *Kunstformen*, see "Form in music" above, p. 71.

[12] As in the old adage: "Dulcia pro patria mori."

confirmed with a {259} cry of triumph amid the salvos of trumpets and drums, even more reverently than before – all this needs to be heard. In a magnificent turn of events hinging on one decisive move, the main *Satz* stands before us again, image of mourning that no word of consolation can extinguish.

But note what now becomes of the funeral march's narrow idea!

Its theme turns immediately to the subdominant (for the second time! – so serious is the mood). And here a sublimely earnest discussion ensues; three voices exchange their views, of which only one (the middle voice in Example 5.26) reminds us of the Second Part, whereas the others (whose content is heard immediately prior to the example[13]) bring something completely new.

Example 5.26

The discussion strides forth in the form of a strict triple fugue, ranges far and wide, gradually draws all the voices into the fray, and intensifies into a passionate struggle in which everyone ultimately reels, seeking each other out with weapons drawn. —Could victory *yet* be the final stage of the hero's career?— The struggle falls silent before the voice of grief, which confusedly ventures onto the dominant and is struck dumb—and then, after soothing and stilling the passionately sudden uproar of all the voices, spurred on by their pain, it sings its sublimely immortal song to all those submerged in blood and darkness; until that too is extinguished.—

Had Beethoven sung his heroic poem after the demise of his hero, had he seen this Briareus of the hundred thousand arms, for whom the world had become too small, so narrowly confined in his exile on St.

---

13 I am assuming that this is what Marx means; he actually says: "die ihren Inhalt unmittelbar vorher gegeben." Even my interpretation is not strictly true – although the top voice is heard a few bars before Marx's abstracted example, the sixteenth-note motive of the bottom voice is not in evidence.

Helena, then perhaps even this second act (who can measure such things?) might have become for him a yet deeper revelation; the conclusion of the work would perforce have been wondrously fashioned, if it had been fashioned at all. But his task was not thus defined; he beheld his hero in the midst of a warrior's career. This determines the course of the drama.

The hero and his victory, the victory and its deathly toll {260} – such is *not* the final goal: that is reserved for *peace*. This is how Beethoven must have viewed it, no matter how Napoleon thought about it.

The *third act*, the so-called Scherzo, opens up its own perspective. In the teeming activity of the string choir, both intensely rhythmic, as if thousands were stepping together, and yet very hushed, there seem to be massed armies – to maintain the image from the Idea of the whole – drawing together endlessly. But not to battle – for a single oboe, hidden high above the rest, unexpectedly mixes its brisk song with their tuneless approach. One seems to recognize some bold folk tune or soldier's song from that time.

Allegro vivace

Example 5.27

And this commotion runs along, almost without end and always in a secret hush, until the song finally breaks out rejoicing with the noise of trumpets and the voices of the entire orchestra; set free beyond a care, it builds to a willful close.

Is this the fervor of camp life? Is it peace, with the army marching off toward its beloved homeland? The sound of the horns already drifts over with buoyant courage, like nimble riders on their steeds:

Example 5.28

The troops behold them with satisfaction, shouting encouragement. And then the horns split up, teasing each other, and lose themselves in an excess of spirit, all the way up to their highest, penetrating, e♭2. To this the strains of country round dances from the homeland join in, with the graceful flattery of a young bride! Again the horns chime in and again they move playfully around each other, except that a sound of longing and desire enters in, {261} namely, the seldom used seventh, D♭ (written, in the horn parts, as B♭), on natural horns – for Beethoven was not familiar with our emasculated valve horns.

Example 5.29

And now – perhaps the general has dismissed his troops – everyone rushes off to the joys and celebrations of peace; this is the fourth act. The theme that we have already found in two works[14] appears here in its full significance. Has its harmless charm remained in Beethoven's mind ever since his Prometheus ballet? Is it a folk tune? — We do not know these things, nor do we now wish to follow the graceful games taken up by the theme, nor to listen to the prayer of thanks arising from its innocent tones. It is not our task to exhaust all the details but rather to mark the essential moments of the whole.

Thus the heroic consecration of Napoleon and of Beethoven.

THE "EROICA" SYMPHONY AND IDEAL MUSIC

The heroic symphony, which has held our attention for so long already, is not merely one great work among others; in addition, it initiates a new era for the arts and, as far as we can judge from all the evidence within music and outside of it, it is definitive for the realm of musical art. For it is that work in which musical art – without allying itself with the poet's word or the dramatist's plot – autonomously and with an autonomous work first leaves the play of formation and of vague excitations and feelings for the sphere of more lucid and determined consciousness,

---

[14] Marx refers here to his discussion of the ballet *The Creatures of Prometheus*, where he notes that the theme of its finale was used by Beethoven in an earlier Contradanse, in the "Eroica" Variations, Op. 35, and in the finale of the "Eroica" Symphony. Marx, *Beethoven*, p. 206.

in which it comes of age, now placing itself, as a peer, in the circle of its sister arts. This progress cannot be superseded; it can only be further pursued, with greater or lesser success, within the newly attained sphere.

Formative play, that blessedly playful life [*spielseliges Leben*] of tones, should not be discounted in the least over and against [music's] progression into {262} another sphere. Beethoven above all, before him Mozart, Haydn, and Bach, and all other musical artists before and after Beethoven in the field of instrumental music, have been happily dependent on it. Play that serves as its own self-satisfied goal and purpose is different from work directed toward a distinct goal that lies outside of itself, and has its own profound significance in all the arts and in human existence overall. The pleasing play of rhyme and meter in poetry has often been regarded in itself as poetry, just as the play of tones has stood for all of music, for the only true music. The painter, with an auspicious smile and a freely unaccountable mood, is at play in the bright alternation of colors, in the breezy surge of branches and leaves and clouds, and in the fantastical connections of his arabesques ... The play of tones is the *primal music* [*Urmusik*], it was and ever will be the mother lode from which everything that lives in music draws its lifeblood, its existence.

And yet man, consigned through his mortality to limitation, to goal and purpose, cannot play on with no end or purpose in sight, even in art. Above all else, Man seeks himself in his play; play should be His play and should carry the stamp and expression of His existence, as He feels it, and as He himself feels in any given moment.[15] In the play of tones, man's fantasy seeks as well the *feeling* of his existence; it poeticizes the feeling of a specific moment in his existence that he is just now living or has lived. The play of tones is no longer without goal and purpose; it directs itself toward this more or less sharply determined point that the musical master sets as his goal. {263} This play remains free only in so far as the setting of the goal abstains from the sharpness of actual purposiveness or of exact science. In this way a swarm of bees moves off without goal or direction, unconscious of a whither; and it swarms around a fragrantly attractive flower-bed in free but ever more determined circles, just as tones ramble in unfettered play and flock to the specific frame of

---

[15] The capital letters are Marx's; they would seem to put man in the role normally assigned to the Creator, thus linking artistic creation with the original act of creation. This supports James Hepokoski's reading of Marx's view of artistic creativity, as put forth in "Masculine–feminine," *The Musical Times* 135 (August 1994), 494.

mind in which creative fantasy is pleased to immerse itself. Whatever suggested this specific direction to fantasy in the first place is immaterial – whether it was a preordained text or some other determination from outside, some still lingering mood or the memory of one, or some other no longer determinable impetus. Enough of this; the directive to enter into the new sphere of musical art has been given, and it is humanly necessary. For man is only what he feels himself to be: in real life he feels in accordance with the impress of circumstances; in art his fantasy projects circumstances and moods. This is again a form of play, for the circumstances and their consequences are not really assigned from outside; they are freely created in the formative spirit – in the imagination, within which the spirit forms and shapes.[16] But insofar as man fashions the pressing circumstances and moods of real life into art, he feels himself to be the master of this self-created world, and in its transfiguring reflection he feels redeemed and freed from the real world. In this resides the ecstasy of artistic creation and the consolation of art, its power of renewal for all those willing to receive it ...

> With examples taken from the literary arts, Marx argues that art does not excite actual feelings but rather brings them before the imagination.

{264} But now the last step had to be taken. And Beethoven was called to take it.

Man himself was to become the content of his musical art – and there are many men, not merely an I, but also a You.

His feeling was to present itself to his inner intuition – and there are various feelings that exclude each other, making their appearance in isolation, but which, through a psychological, natural, and necessary evolution, can also conjure up a progressive image of life. This happens surely not with the pragmatic certainty of the word (and is even that so certain?), but rather only in flickering outlines and colors, like the reflection of reality in water or in a mirage; yet it is so much more artistic and artistically effective, the confidant not of inexorably confining exactitude but of the charming play of fantasy.

With this, music took upon itself the twofold task of becoming both dramatic and objective ...

---

[16] "... sie sind frei im bildenden Geist – in der Einbildung, in dem in ihm selber vorgehenden Bilden oder Gestalten des Geistes – geschaffene." This is a troubling passage; I am not entirely sure what the "ihm" is supposed to refer to.

There follows a brief discussion of programmatic music before Beethoven.

{265} All these things were preludes, preliminary preparations, if one looks away from individual artists to that which is achieved through them: the continually productive power and destiny of art to move forward and elaborate itself. That which happened only experimentally, peripherally, and by leaning on extramusical props, now needed to be brought to fulfillment in real, autonomous, and free-standing artworks. Only then did music become objective and ideal, this latter in the sense that it portrayed, with its own means, life itself, namely, entire states of life in accordance with the *Idea*, in accordance with the spiritually transfigured image begotten in the artist.

This was the work of Beethoven …

His sonatas … offered more than just one image of the coherent and true-to-nature life of the soul; they offered a whole series of necessary events in the course of such a life, as inwardly unified and necessary as any poem or painting. In his Hero's Symphony we have before us an ideal image – not a general state of soul, common to many, but rather a lofty, rare, and {266} wholly specific life process; we have stepped from the lyric to the epic.[17] And, indeed, this is not just opinion, presumption, or construction (one might provisionally take it as such in the case of those sonatas); in the "Eroica" it is the historically authentic, unshakable will of one who has dared to take the step.

"But is this step possible?"

Above all, it is already a great deed for Beethoven to have dared the step, even were it to prove unfeasible. For he thus granted the urge of the human spirit toward self-consciousness and toward world-consciousness within its circle of life …

"But even so, we ask again, isn't music, in its inability to define objects, unsuited for the revelation of objective content? Doesn't this content reside in mere superscripts and – in your subjective imagination, in that which you arbitrarily imagine with or alongside the music?"

Our subjective imagination? —One ought well consider, just whom this "your" embraces! No less than all the great musical artists, acknowledged as such even by you yourself, from Bach and Händel (one need

---

[17] See note 7 above.

only read the works and their verbal elucidations – or the *Maigruss!*[18]) up
to the present day. They all have been able to find that capability in their
art and have built their life's calling upon it. Or – if you dare to say it –
they were all fools, misguided in their own field of expertise.

We will gladly make the confession here that the inscription, the
naming of the work, prepares us to comprehend its content. We call this
avowal a confession[19] because those who doubt the capability of music
for more definite content will eagerly tender the assertion that such a
capability resides {267} only in the superscription. At the same time, no
one would believe us for a second if we changed inscriptions, calling, say,
the "Eroica" Symphony the "Pastoral" and the "Pastoral" the "Eroica,"
just as no musician thought anything of the superscription "Didone
abbandonata" when Clementi, reminiscing over his days in the parterre,
once gave this name to a sonata, or would think anything of superscriptions used by virtuosi, such as "Souvenir de Berlin," etc.

It goes without saying that superscriptions are important as a first
clue, since they give the presuppositions for the content of the artwork;
but this content must itself then follow. Yet this is not a particular need of
music's: that one familiarize oneself, no matter how, with an art work's
subject and its presuppositions before one approaches an artwork, is an
indispensable condition for all the arts, in hundreds upon hundreds of
works. Who could comprehend an Assumption of Mary or Raphael's
Transfiguration were the events that the painter desired to portray not
known to him from the Bible or from legend? …

> At this point Marx interrupts his argument to present and then give a
> critique of Richard Wagner's programmatic interpretation of the
> "Eroica." He argues that Wagner's reading is in fact too abstract, that it is
> but an "intellectual extract" of the teeming life of the symphony.

{270} "Setting aside the program and all peripheral verbiage, where
finally are the music's means for determinate expression? Leaving the
authority of the artist out of the picture, how should we others understand their expression?"

We must respond: direct your search to art – to its material, the
sounds, chords, tonal relations (some few letters from her alphabet have
already appeared here), rhythms! Take to this task all the aids of simile,

---

[18] See note 1 above.

[19] Marx puns here with *Geständniss* (avowal) and *Zugeständniss* (confession).

symbol, psychological coherence, all these spiritual guidelines that no artist and no person can do without! You abstract philosophers of art, you who have confined your perhaps natively receptive characters within the stocks of abstract understanding, do not so limit yourselves by holding to the threads of a system that, spider-like, you have drawn out from your own selves, but turn instead toward works of art! Nestle within them, impel yourselves toward art in the strength of your faith, as did the patriarch who at one time struggled with the spirit – "I will not leave you until you bless me!" was his incessant, prayerful cry – and to whom was shown Jacob's ladder, upon which the angels of heaven bore their blessed embassy down and then back up again! No other directive can be given you *here*. Here there is no teaching, but only a telling, of that which has happened and has been beheld …

> Marx concludes this chapter with a critique of the interpretations of the "Eroica" by Schindler, Oulibicheff, and Fétis.

THE FUTURE BEFORE THE TRIBUNAL OF THE PAST

{278} This time it was the "Eroica" Symphony that was to approach the tribunal; "she's not the first!" Mephistopheles says to a despairing Faust.[20]

It is only natural that the new enters into an uncomfortable relation with the old; sprouting buds give dried up leaves their last push off the branch. This process is so simple in the course of nature that its inevitability and its advantage are readily and generally recognized.

Not so in the life of the spirit. When the new idea comes to face the old, which up to now has filled and ruled its sphere of influence, this latter has in no way fulfilled its vocation or consumed its life energy; instead, it lives on amid the broad reach of human existence, in thousands upon thousands of individuals and in thousands of circumstances, continues to be effective in their minds and in accordance with their needs, and thus has not merely been valid up to now, but rather is valid still, or perhaps forever. And yet the necessity of progress stirs beside it and pushes against it, striving to stake a claim over and against the old, first through isolated individuals and then through ever increasing numbers. {279} This necessity is not a force that intrudes from somewhere

---

[20] Mephistopheles is referring to Faust's corruption of Gretchen, in Goethe, *Faust*, Part I.

outside, however; it is the urge of a hitherto one-sided idea toward its other side, the urge to draw its consequences from all sides and live through them. This is what lends the struggle of ideas and principles its venomous edge; one feels blood relations on both sides and is at once embarrassed by and provoked to a fight with one's own flesh and blood.

This uneasy and never resting process of the spirit is its history. Every idea at the height of its rule becomes a King Lear, who watches the same forces that formed his own power and sovereignty grow up in his children and finally revolt against him. On page 175 we attempted to pursue the natural process of the spirit through three stages of musical evolution, and it was perforce shown that the progression to the next stage did not abrogate the right of the previous stage; the play of tones remained and remains warranted alongside the stage that reflects the movements of emotion [*Gemüt*], and this langauge of the soul maintains its right to our hearts alongside the ideal tendencies that first appeared independently in the heroic symphony.

Each side of the divide possesses its right; but what it does not possess is the ability to acknowledge the right of the other side. The lower stages can be surveyed from the higher standpoint, but not vice versa; and it is also easier to approve of the superseded standpoint, for one has lived through it oneself, than to comprehend the progress away from it, provided one was not prone to an immediate alliance with such progress.

Beethoven had already experienced this. In spite of some small japes at tone painting he had no trouble justly acknowledging Haydn's merits, while the obviously good-natured Haydn had not been in a position to follow the first jolt toward progress in Beethoven's C minor Trio.[21] One must keep this in mind, in order to bear contrariety with composure, even when it comes on in an unruly and hardheaded fashion.

And thus the great step had now been taken. How was it received?

Above all, it was not recognized; one felt oneself on the beaten path, and anything that pushed one off it was held to be a mere passing shock – whether through inadvertence, clumsiness, or {280} spite, who knows? Beethoven's own student, Ries, at a rehearsal of that famous horn entry [Example 5.30] cried out: "That sounds just awful!" – he thought the horn had come in wrong – and almost had his ears boxed by the master.

---

[21] Op. 1, No. 3, to which Haydn professed himself to be lukewarm.

Example 5.30

Much later still (in his and Wegeler's 1838 biographical notes on Beet-hoven) he says of the same spot: "In this very allegro there is a nasty whim of Beethoven's for the horn" – he thus sees the passage as a ca-price.

In a report from Vienna appearing in the *Allgemeine musikalische Zeit-ung*, we read how the Viennese critics received the work: "[The "Ero-ica"] is actually a very broadly executed, bold, and wild fantasy. It is not lacking in strikingly beautiful passages, but quite often seems to lose itself in irregularity. There is too much of the lurid and bizarre, which makes an overview difficult and almost entirely loses the sense of unity. The Eberl symphony was again extraordinarily pleasing." One sees that the reporter did not exactly lack good will; but he has had a hard time gaining an overview of the work, and the actual intention of the work has remained completely hidden from him. He declares its striking as-pects to be lurid, bizarre, and irregular, without asking if there existed a particular motivation for these things. He felt better only upon hearing the Eberl symphony. How lucky of him to run into it there, in order to help him place the Beethoven symphony in the correct light! Who today knows anything anymore about Eberl and his symphonies?

But where is the actual error in all these remarks? Nowhere else but in the fact that the new work is judged according to aims and precepts that are not its own. The questions for reviewers are as follows:

What is the determining aim [*Bestimmung*] of the work?

What can be judged from this aim?

How has it been worked toward?

In other words, first the discussion of end, then the discussion of means. Why would anyone want to judge the latter without the former, or, worse yet, to foist the wrong end upon the means?

Those critics did not inquire after Beethoven's goal and aim. Unaware that another standpoint had been put into place they held fast to that {281} of the play of tones and, in any case, to that of the subjective music of feeling (see p. 175). But the play of tones lives above all in the graceful alternation of forms, in that it flatters the senses, now enticing,

182 Hermeneutic Analysis and the *Idee*

now delighting them, and excites the half conscious, half sleeping spirit, only to relax it again ... And the sphere of subjective feeling is also satisfied in the quieter, gentler regions – although even beloved Mozart and profound Bach have given many a shock to those critics and to the aesthetic of taste and beauty. Thus it is hardly surprising that the offense taken at Beethoven was great – and still makes itself felt today.

If Oulibicheff reports the truth, Ries finds his chief successor in Berlioz, who says of the famous passage in the horn:

> The tremolo of the first and second violins alone maintains the notes b♭ and a♭, [i.e.] the incomplete seventh chord b♭–d–f–a♭; and now a horn, seeming to mistake its place and come in two bars too early, rashly enters with the beginning of the main theme, which rests exclusively on the chord e♭–g–b♭. One understands what a disturbing impression this melody of the tonic chord (e♭–g–b♭) must perforce make against the dissonant tones (b♭–a♭) of the dominant chord.[22]

Only Lenz has understood this well ("it is some distant echo of the motive of the Allegro that hovers there, lost, *in gurgite vasto*"),[23] even though the horn is not exactly an echo, but rather, on the wide battlefield Beethoven envisions here, a strange summons drifting entirely out of a lost distance, not at all belonging to the present moment but auguring and heralding those to follow – namely, the return of the heroic theme after the struggle seemed extinct.

To men of the profession, moreover, Beethoven's derring-do is not wholly unheard of; they know that, in the case of an anticipation, a tone {282} from a future chord is taken in advance and added to a chord in which it does not at all belong (see A in Example 5.31). Consequently they will even accept double anticipations, as in B and C, even though they appear with twice the harshness, by introducing two tones that contradict the prevailing chord.

Example 5.31

Now: Beethoven, too, introduces just two contradictory tones, e♭–g, against b♭–a♭. Only his contradiction is decisive, for here a complete

[22] Hector Berlioz, *A travers chants* (Paris: Gründ, 1971), 41–42.
[23] Wilhelm von Lenz, *Beethoven et ses trois styles* (repr. New York: Da Capo Press, 1980), 87.

chord clearly and unmistakably intrudes on another. But this is not "the laughing of the chimera," [24] as Lenz (enchanted by Beethoven's originality) puts it, but rather the power of an epic idea that is waiting to be discerned here.

Oulibicheff finds something similar in bars 276–79 (bars 2–5 below):

Example 5.32

… Oulibicheff perceives two interlocked chords here: … "four bars in which the flutes set a high e against the high f, while the strings strike the chord c–e in the depths, which has as a consequence the juxtaposition of two key centers (*tonalités*), A minor and F major. One is indeed aware of the chord of the major seventh, f–a–c–e; but this latter is only an apparent chord, an extended dissonance, which as such is subjected to a necessary [resolution] and which has nothing in common with Beethoven's *double chord*, which is neither prepared nor resolved."[25]

First of all, this grammatical analysis is incorrect; in the following example, the harmony {283} is seen to be prepared at A and resolved step by step at B.

Example 5.33

Oulibicheff simply did not notice this, because both the register and the placement of the instruments – namely the flutes on f3–e3 – made too

[24] Ibid.
[25] Oulibicheff, *Beethoven*, 184–85.

sharp an impression on him. But this is not about his or anyone else's analysis; one grants him the grating effect of such conflicting sounds, for the outcry of battlefield rage must find expression at some time or other. Berlioz is completely correct when he says, of a similar passage: "one can hardly suppress a tremor of terror at this portrait of indomitable rage. It is the voice of despair, almost of frenzy."[26] Indeed, Oulibicheff himself hears a death rattle here, expressed with that "truth too true" that in the realm of art becomes a lie (has he never seen the possessed ones in Raphael's *Transfiguration* or read *Lear* and *Othello* and Shylock and Aeschylus and Dante?).[27]

And here we have the whole aesthetics of good taste, perched on the Curulian elder's stool![28]

Even a harmless modulatory shock falls under suspicion – as if everything walked in a straight line during a battle.

In the Third Part, namely, where the victory is already assured and everything is aburst with domineering courage and joyfulness, and where smiles and flattery hang from everyone's lips, an appendix (the same that motivated the repeat of the First Part and the entrance of the Second Part) quietly brings back the leading idea, the hero's word, which is now relaxed [*atemschöpfend*] but soaring.

Example 5.34

---

[26] But Berlioz is in fact talking about this very passage. See Berlioz, *A travers chants*, 41.

[27] Oulibicheff, *Beethoven*, 177.

[28] In Grimm's Dictionary there is a short note on this; it refers to some sort of chair on which village elders sat in judgement.

{284} Then the orchestra repeats it in D♭ with a mighty and unmediated jolt, lets that echo away on the concord of D♭ and then blasts its way into C, again with the greatest power and just as little mediation: The word *shall* prevail! And it has triumphed! And it shall triumph and rule! How natural and comprehensible this would have had to be to Oulibicheff, for whom the battle [in this movement] was vivid! He indeed understood it – if only there were no such thing as grammar (dilettantes often parade it, as does Lenz, who has the utmost contempt for form and technique but then takes great pains about the form, namely about a chimerical Allegretto form) and the ear, i.e. taste! For Oulibicheff, Beethoven goes immediately from E♭ to D♭, then D♭ to C, "without worrying in the least about the obvious octaves and hidden fifths which then obtain [Oh!! – it's not even true]. I confess that this is not very pleasant for the ear, but the poetic idea comes to the aid of the musical idea here, or, better, it takes its place." The so-called poetic Idea treated as if it were an assistant called in when the music is in trouble! Thus the natural relationship, in which the Idea conditions the means of its realization, is turned on its head. Further on he adds: "this is strange but striking [*frappant*] ... From this example and thousands of others we can draw the highly notable and yet too little noted lesson that things flawed in and of themselves can be transformed into things of relative beauty through the introduction of a poetic idea or a specific program."[29]

And we are still not done with Oulibicheff; we would not need to mention him so often if this same fundamental view of things did not continue to shackle the majority of art lovers and art philosophers. Here our objection is not even concerned chiefly with him but with an assertion. The last passage he abstracts is the following fragment from the finale:

[29] Oulibicheff, *Beethoven*, 178–79.

Example 5.35

{285} This is found to be "astonishing on paper" (again the harmonic foundation, anticipation and suspension, is very simple, and the piercing quality resides only in the manner of portrayal – see Example 5.36), "yet it goes by so quickly in performance that the ear is hardly jolted or else lays the blame on the performers."[30]

Example 5.36

Such things are not of the essence, as has already been said above. The question is always: what is the sense and purpose of the passage?[31]

Beethoven's finale has appeared to us to be an image of peace, which ultimately must be the goal of all war. The happiness of the people – or, in Beethoven's sense, of humanity – plays out in peacefully rustic games; the warriors have returned to their hearths. But the energy that alone ensures peace, by being always prepared for war, does not slumber. This energy is felt in many places but is especially prominent in a section in C minor, beginning in bar 117. Here the first violin, framed by other voices, introduces the theme of the finale as a fugue subject, the second violin answers, violas and basses complete the exposition, and a discus-

[30] Ibid., 186–87.

[31] Marx uses the word *Satz* here, and elsewhere in this chapter, in contexts where he clearly is not referring to anything like a formal *Satz*. Thus I have here swerved from my policy of leaving the word *Satz* untranslated.

sion on the subject ensues, as more and more voices eagerly join in. The zeal grows more passionate, culminates in the above passage (Example 5.35) – which one might call contentious – and then turns again, amid the anxious urgings of the violin and the cajoling tones of the flute, toward childlike play and joy.

But if one asks us about the necessity of this process and of a hundred other details, we shall answer with good cheer that we are in no way capable of showing how every feature of an ideal artwork follows necessarily from the Idea of the whole or what its exact significance is for the whole – because this absolute necessity, this significance that would pervade every individual detail, does not exist in any artwork, because it would be antithetical even to the fundamental character of art, namely that blessed play to which Beethoven, above all, gladly surrendered, just as he remained, through all the exalted hours and bitter suffering, always the childlike and all too readily cheerful man. (As an opportune example, note the charming dalliance with the theme at A and the innocent joy of the flute [at B]:) {286}

Example 5.37

Yet in the end, to speak with Mozart, music will always be music. We summon it up to express our Idea and, sure enough, it comes – but as its own essence, possessing its own life and its own unimpeachable right. It is no different for painters: no sooner do they wish to paint the saints, or the queen of heaven, to make visible the Idea of a saint or the mother of God, then every useless limb and article of clothing and background matter claims its right to be there, and no one may question their significance:

> In the end, we yet depend
> On the creatures we created.
>
> [Am Ende hängen wir doch ab
> Von Kreaturen, die wir machten.]

SELECT BIBLIOGRAPHY

Bauer, Elisabeth Eleonore. *Wie Beethoven auf den Sockel kam: Die Entstehung eines musikalischen Mythos.* Stuttgart and Weimar: J. B. Metzler, 1992

Bent, Ian. *Analysis.* London: Macmillan, 1987

Music Analysis in the Nineteenth Century. 2 vols. Cambridge: Cambridge University Press, 1994

"The 'compositional process' in music theory 1713–1850." *Music Analysis* 3 (1984), 29–55

Bonds, Mark Evan. *Wordless Rhetoric: Musical Form and the Metaphor of the Oration.* Cambridge MA: Harvard University Press, 1991

Burnham, Scott. "A. B. Marx and the gendering of sonata form." In *Music Theory in the Age of Romanticism*, ed. Ian Bent. Cambridge: Cambridge University Press, 1996. Pp. 163–86

"Aesthetics, theory and history in the works of Adolph Bernhard Marx." Ph.D. dissertation, Brandeis University, 1988

Beethoven Hero. Princeton: Princeton University Press, 1995

"Criticism, faith, and the *Idee*: A. B. Marx's early reception of Beethoven." *19th-Century Music* 8/3 (Spring 1990), 183–92

"The role of sonata form in A. B. Marx's theory of form." *Journal of Music Theory* 33/2 (Fall 1989), 247–71

Dahlhaus, Carl. "Ästhetische Prämissen der 'Sonatenform' bei Adolf Bernhard Marx." *Archiv für Musikwissenschaft* 41 (1984), 73–85

"Formenlehre und Gattungstheorie bei A. B. Marx." In *Heinrich Sievers zum 70. Geburtstag*, ed. Gunter Katzenberger. Tutzing: Hans Schneider, 1978. Pp. 29–35

"Gefühlsästhetik und musikalische Formenlehre." *Deutsche Vierteljahrsschrift für Literaturwissenschaft und Geistesgeschichte* 41 (1967), 505–16

"Geschichte als Problem der Musiktheorie: Über einige Berliner Musiktheoretiker des 19. Jahrhunderts." In *Studien zur Musikgeschichte Berlins im frühen 19. Jahrhundert*, ed. Carl Dahlhaus. Regensburg: Bosse, 1980. Pp. 405–13

189

Die Musiktheorie im 18. und 19. Jahrhundert. Erster Teil: Grundzüge einer Systematik. Geschichte der Musiktheorie, ed. Friederich Zaminer, vol. 10. Darmstadt: Wissenschaftliche Buchgesellschaft, 1984.

"Some models of unity in musical form." *Journal of Music Theory* 19 (Spring 1975), 2–30

Dehn, Siegfried Wilhelm. *Theoretisch-praktische Harmonielehre.* Berlin, 1840

Edler, Arnfried. "Zur Musikanschauung von Adolf Bernhard Marx." In *Beiträge zur Geschichte der Musikanschauung im 19. Jahrhundert*, ed. W. Salmen. Regensburg: Bosse, 1965. Pp. 103–12

Eicke, Kurt-Erich. *Der Streit zwischen Adolph Bernhard Marx und Gottfried Wilhelm Fink um die Kompositionslehre.* Regensburg: Gustav Bosse Verlag, 1966

Fellerer, Karl Gustav. "Adolf Bernhard Marx und Gottfried Wilhelm Fink." In *Festschrift Alfred Orel*, ed. Hellmut Federhofer. Vienna: Rudolf M. Rohrer, 1960. Pp. 59–65

Fink, Gottfried Wilhelm. *Der neumusikalische Lehrjammer oder Beleuchtung der Schrift: Die alte Musiklehre im Streit mit unserer Zeit.* Leipzig, 1842

Forchert, Arno. "Adolf Bernhard Marx und seine *Berliner allgemeine musikalische Zeitung.*" In *Studien zur Musikgeschichte Berlins im frühen 19. Jahrhundert.* Pp. 381–404

Kirchmeyer, Helmut. "Ein Kapitel Adolf Bernhard Marx. Über Sendungsbewußtsein und Bildungsstand der Berliner Musikkritik zwischen 1824 und 1830." In *Beiträge zur Geschichte der Musikanschauung im 19. Jahrhundert.* Pp. 73–101

Logier, J. B. *System der Musik-Wissenschaft und der praktischen Composition.* Transl. A. B. Marx. Berlin, 1827

Marx, Adolph Bernhard. *Allgemeine Musiklehre.* Leipzig: Breitkopf und Härtel, 1839

Die alte Musiklehre im Streit mit unserer Zeit. Leipzig: Breitkopf und Härtel, 1841

Erinnerungen: Aus meinem Leben. 2 vols. Berlin: Otto Janke, 1865

"Die Form in der Musik." In *Die Wissenschaften im neunzehnten Jahrhundert*, ed. Dr. J. A. Romberg, vol. 2. Leipzig: Romberg's Verlag, 1856. Pp. 21–48

Die Lehre von der musikalischen Komposition, praktisch-theoretisch. 4 vols. Vol. 1. 7th edn. Leipzig: Breitkopf und Härtel, 1868

Die Lehre von der musikalischen Komposition, praktisch-theoretisch. 4 vols. Vol. 3: *Die angewandte Kompositionslehre.* 2nd edn, 1848; 4th edn, 1868. Leipzig: Breitkopf und Härtel

Ludwig van Beethoven: Leben und Schaffen. 2 vols. 3rd edn, ed. Dr. Gustav Behncke. Berlin: Verlag von Otto Janke, 1875

Moyer, Birgitte. "Concepts of musical form in the nineteenth century with special reference to A. B. Marx and sonata form." Ph.D. dissertation, Stanford University, 1969

Nägeli, Hans Georg. *Vorlesungen über Musik mit Berücksichtigung der Dilettanten.* Stuttgart: Cotta, 1826

Oulibicheff, Aléxandre. *Beethoven, ses critiques, ses glossateurs.* Paris: Gavelot and Leipzig: F. A. Brockhaus, 1857

Pederson, Sanna. "A. B. Marx, Berlin concert life, and German national identity." *19th-Century Music* 18/2 (Fall, 1994), 87–107

Ritzel, Fred. *Die Entwicklung der 'Sonatenform' im musiktheoretischen Schrifttum des 18. und 19. Jahrhunderts.* 2nd edn. Neue musikgeschichtliche Forschungen, ed. Lothar Hoffmann-Erbrecht, vol. 1. Wiesbaden: Breitkopf und Härtel, 1969

Rummenhöller, Peter. "Der idealistisch-pragmatische Theoriebegriff Adolph Bernhard Marx." In *Musiktheoretisches Denken im 19. Jahrhundert*, ed. Peter Rummenhöller. Studien zur Musikgeschichte des 19. Jahrhunderts, vol. 12. Regensburg: Bosse, 1967. Pp. 29–35

Salomon, Ora Frischberg. *Beethoven's Symphonies and J. S. Dwight: the Birth of American Music Criticism.* Boston: Northeastern University Press, 1995

Schmalfeldt, Janet. "Form as the process of becoming: the Beethoven-Hegelian tradition and the 'Tempest' Sonata." *Beethoven Forum* 4 (1995), 37–71

Sipe, Thomas. "Interpreting Beethoven: History, Aesthetics, and Critical Reception." Ph.D. dissertation, University of Pennsylvania, 1992

Sowa, Georg. *Anfänge institutioneller Musikerziehung in Deutschland (1800–1843): Pläne, Realisierung und zeitgenössische Kritik.* Studien zur Musikgeschichte des 19. Jahrhunderts, vol. 33. Regensburg: Bosse, 1973

Thaler, Lotte. *Organische Form in der Musiktheorie des 19. und beginnenden 20. Jahrhunderts.* Berliner musikwissenschaftlichen Arbeiten, ed. Carl Dahlhaus and Rudolf Stephan, vol. 25. Munich: Katzbichler, 1984

Wallace, Robin. *Beethoven's Critics: Aesthetic Dilemmas and Resolutions during the Composer's Lifetime.* Cambridge: Cambridge University Press, 1986

Weber, Gottfried. *Versuch einer geordneten Theorie der Tonsetzkunst.* 3 vols. 3rd edn. Mainz: B. Schott's Söhne, 1830–32

Ziolkowski, Theodore. *German Romanticism and its Institutions.* Princeton: Princeton University Press, 1990

INDEX

DATE DUE

Demco, Inc. 38-293